FRANCOIS MAURIAC
by

MAXWELL A. SMITH

The book treats Mauriac, winner of the Nobel Prize for Literature in 1952, primarily as a novelist and dramatist, since it seems likely that his enduring claim to greatness lies in these two fields. In the discussion of his life, particular attention has been paid to his childhood and youth, for this formative period is of paramount importance, representing as it does the rich storehouse of memories for settings and characters in all his novels and dramas. Special importance has been given to the literary influences Mauriac has undergone, documented with quotations from his memoirs and essays which aid us in understanding his own character and inspiration. This writer finds three predominate themes running through all Mauriac's work: the tension and conflict in his own person between passionate love of nature and religious faith; the desperate loneliness of the individual unable to communicate with others; and finally the satire of bourgeois smugness, social conformity and lack of Christian compassion. In spite of the valid criticism of Mauriac for his dark pessimism this writer finds Mauriac likely to occupy a permanent and distinguished place in the history of French fiction as a penetrating analyst of character, a master of dramatic narration, but above all as a great stylist and prose poet.

e

7

, Emeritus

es

TWAYNE'S WORLD AUTHORS SERIES (TWAS)

The purpose of TWAS is to survey the major writers —novelists, dramatists, historians, poets, philosophers, and critics—of the nations of the world. Among the national literatures covered are those of Australia, Canada, China, Eastern Europe, France, Germany, Greece, India, Italy, Japan, Latin America, New Zealand, Poland, Russia, Scandinavia, Spain, and the African nations, as well as Hebrew, Yiddish, and Latin Classical literatures. This survey is complemented by Twayne's United States Authors Series and English Authors Series.

The intent of each volume in these series is to present a critical-analytical study of the works of the writer; to include biographical and historical material that may be necessary for understanding, appreciation, and critical appraisal of the writer; and to present all material in clear, concise English—but not to vitiate the scholarly content of the work by doing so.

François Mauriac

By MAXWELL A. SMITH

The Florida State University

Twayne Publishers, Inc.   ::   New York

To Mary Clyde

ABOUT THE AUTHOR

A native of Madison, Wis., Dr. Smith received his AB and MA at the Univ. of Wisconsin, and Docteur de l'Université de Paris. He has taught at Univ. of Wis., the Sorbonne, U.C.L.A., Univ. of Virginia, Univ. of Chattanooga (Dean and Guerry Professor of French); and since 1965 has been Visiting Professor in Mod. Lang. at Florida State Univ. His honors include Past President South Atlantic Mod. Lang. Assoc., Past Pres. Academic Deans of Southern States, Chevalier of French Legion of Honor. Contributor to the French Review and Modern Language Journal and others. Among his books published are *L'Influence des Lakistes sur les Romantiques français, A Short History of French Literature, Knight of the Air (Antoine de Saint-Exupéry); Jean Giono* and many school editions of French texts. He was the first Lecteur Américain in the new department of American Literature at the Sorbonne, Univ. of Paris, 1918-20.

Preface

In addition to my discussion of Mauriac's life as background for his writings, I have limited this book primarily to a consideration of his fiction and drama for two compelling reasons: first, because it is in these two fields, particularly the former, that his enduring claim to greatness lies; second, because even in these two domains Mauriac has shown such fecundity—twenty novels, two volumes of short stories, four full-length plays—that any treatment of his other and I think more ephemeral writings would impinge upon space needed for discussion in depth of the novelist and dramatist. While I shall not treat as such Mauriac's biographies, memoirs, political and religious essays, or literary criticism, I have read most of these and have drawn on them extensively for material related to my biography and analysis of his literary achievement.

The reader may perhaps wonder why more space has been devoted in biography to Mauriac's childhood and youth than to the following four-and-one-half decades of his life. The reason, of course, is that this formative period is more important for Mauriac, perhaps, than for any other writer since it represents the rich storehouse of memories on which he drew for settings and characters in all his novels and dramas. I can imagine another question on the part of the reader, more difficult to answer. Why have I not adopted a purely chronological treatment of his fiction as so many other critics have done? This would have had one great advantage; namely, the opportunity for dividing his work into two periods (or rather three, treating the early autobiographical novels apart, as indeed I have done), before and after his religious crisis of 1928. If I have not chosen to make this division it is because I agree with North that the novels published after this crisis differ only superficially, not fundamentally, from those written earlier. For the purpose of greater clarity I have decided to discuss Mauriac's mature novels in two groups, the minor novels in one section, the masterpieces in the other. From this point of view a chronological division would not make sense, for great novels and lesser ones alternate in time; in the period before 1928 the successful *Baiser au lépreux* is followed by the mediocre *Fleuve de feu;* in the second period interspersed with weaker novels appear two, perhaps three outstanding works—*Le Noeud de vipères, La Fin de la nuit* and *La Pharisienne.* However arbitrary my division may appear, it has at least the advantage of focusing attention and emphasis on the part of Mauriac's work which seems most likely to endure.

Perhaps the most significant feature of this study is the long chapter on the literary influences which Mauriac has undergone, documented with quotations from his memoirs and essays. It is through a perusal of these statements that one can comprehend and define Mauriac's own character and inspiration, except of course for that indefinable quality of genius which makes him stand out *sui generis* without any disciple or imitator. It is with some temerity and misgiving that as a non-Catholic I have undertaken this study. I am encouraged, however, by the fact that some of Mauriac's least perceptive and most acrimonious critics have been writers of his own faith and that the book on Mauriac which he considers most understanding is by a non-Catholic, Nelly Cormeau. Hopefully also, what the present writer lacks in familiarity with Catholic dogma and theology may be compensated for by a more unfettered and unbiased concentration on Mauriac, not as a Catholic novelist, but as a novelist who incidentally happened also to be a Catholic.

Acknowledgments

I am grateful to the following French, English and American publishers for their kind permission to quote from books by and about François Mauriac.

From Mauriac's works: to Editions Buchet/Chastel for *Le Romancier et ses personnages* and *Les Pages immortelles de Pascal;* to Plon for *La Vie de Jean Racine;* to La Palatine *Ecrits intimes* and *Le Sagouin;* to L'Artisan du Livre for *Le Roman;* to Flammarion for *L'Agneau, Galigaï, Sainte Marguerite de Cortone, Mémoires intérieurs* and *Nouveaux Mémoires intérieurs;* to Editions Bernard Grasset for *Ce que je crois, Dieu et Mammon, Asmodée, Les Mal-Aimés, Le Feu sur la terre,* and for his novels except *L'Agneau, Le Sagouin* and *Galigaï,* and to the British publishers of his novels in English translation, Eyre and Spotteswoode.

From works about Mauriac: to Oxford University Press for *French Novelists of Today* by Henri Peyre; to Editions Buchet/Chastel for *François Mauriac et le problème du romancier catholique* by DuBos; to Gallimard for *Situations I* by Jean-Paul Sartre.

Contents

Chronology

1885   François Mauriac born in Bordeaux, October 11.

1887   Death of father Jean-Paul Mauriac, June 11.

1892   October, enters Marianite school.

1898   Enters Marianite Collège, Grand Lebrun.

1901– Rhetoric class with l'abbé Péquignot.
1902

1904– Obtains *licence* degree, University of Bordeaux.
1905

1906   September, arrives in Paris to prepare for L'Ecole des Chartes.

1908   November, enters L'Ecole des Chartes.

1909   Withdraws to devote himself to literature. November, publishes *Les Mains jointes.*

1910   Praised by Barrès for this first volume of poetry.

1911   First novel, *L'Enfant chargé de chaînes,* appears in *Mercure de France.*

1913   Publication of first novel by Grasset. Marriage with Jeanne Lafont.

1914   Birth of first son and publication of second novel, *La Robe prétexte.*

1914– War service in Red Cross at front and at Salonika. Hos-
1918   pitalized with fever; repatriated in 1918.

1920   Publication of third novel, *La Chair et le sang.*

1921   Publication of fourth novel, *Préséances.*

1922   Great success and instant fame with publication of *Le Baiser au lépreux.*

1922– Period of great fertility; publication of *Le Fleuve de feu,*
1927   *Genitrix, Le Désert de l'amour,* and *Thérèse Desqueyroux.*

1927– Severe religious crisis and attack by André Gide. Publica-
1929   tion of *Destins* in 1928.

1929   Solution of religious crisis; publication of *Ce qui était perdu*.

1932   Election as Président des Gens de Lettres. Publication of *Le Noeud de vipères*. Severe illness and throat operation.

1933   Election to French Academy. Publication of *Le Mystère Frontenac*, an affectionate tribute to his family.

1936   Publication of *La Fin de la nuit* and *Les Anges noirs*. Beginning of Mauriac's journalistic campaign against Franco.

1937   Great success of *Asmodée* at Théâtre Français.

1939   Publication of *Les Chemins de la mer*.

1941   Publication of *La Pharisienne*.

1943   Publication of *Le Cahier noir* by the underground press, expressing his opposition to German occupation.

1944   Resumption of journalistic activity and defense of those accused unjustly of collaboration with the enemy. Support of De Gaulle.

1945–   Return to the theater with *Les mal aimés* (1945), *Passage*
1952   *du Malin* (1948), and *Le Feu sur la terre* (1951). Publication of two novels, *Le Sagouin* (1951) and *Galigaï* (1952).

1952   Selection for the Nobel Prize in Literature.

1954   Publication of his last novel, *L'Agneau*.

1953–   Journalistic support of De Gaulle's policy of independence
1965   for North Africa, on *Le Figaro Littéraire* and for a time, *L'Express*. Beginning of weekly *Bloc-Notes*.

1958   Named Grand Croix de la Légion d'Honneur on recommendation of De Gaulle.

1965   Celebration of his eightieth birthday by a complete issue of *Le Figaro Littéraire*.

1965–   Continuation of his Memoirs with *Nouveaux Mémoires*
1967   *intérieurs* (1965) and *Mémoires politiques* (1967).

1969   Publication of *Un Adolescent d'Autrefois*.

CHAPTER 1

His Life: 1885-1922

"L'enfance est le tout d'une vie, puis-
qu'elle nous en donne la clef." [1]

MANY years ago there taught in a famous university of the
Middle West a professor whose colorful lectures on the
giants of English literature held his students spellbound. One day,
however, a certain brash sophomore had the temerity to approach
him after the class to ask why his lectures never extended beyond
the age of twenty or twenty-one of the authors he discussed. Fix-
ing the student with a glance in which amusement and pity were
mingled, the professor answered: "Because after a writer has
reached this age, what happens later in his life is of little conse-
quence."

Whatever the validity of this sweeping generalization, there is
at least one author, François Mauriac, whom it fits like a glove.
His only published autobiography is entitled *Beginnings of a Life;*
his various volumes of memoirs are filled almost entirely with
these early recollections; and Mauriac confesses that all his novels
were really an attempt to rediscover "this fragrant and sad world
of childhood." [2] Recalling a verse of Henry Bataille, "Adieu mon
enfance! Je vais vivre!" Mauriac comments: "He did not know
that this childhood, to which he was saying farewell, accompanies
us right up to the end, to the day, to the evening, when we shall
say to it 'farewell my childhood, I am going to die.'" [3] But even
then the author will not really be saying good-by to the joy of his
childhood, for he will make his departure, "pressing close in my
arms this poet aged seven."

I Family Background

François Mauriac was born in Bordeaux on October 11, 1885,
the youngest of five children. The eldest, born seven years before,

was his sister Germaine, the only one now surviving and widow of
a professor at the Faculty of Medicine of Bordeaux. The others
were: Raymond who became a lawyer (and under the nom de
plume of Raymond Housilane wrote several novels), Jean who
entered the priesthood and became a *lycée* chaplain, and Pierre
destined later to become Dean of the School of Medicine of the
University of Bordeaux.

François never knew his father Jean-Paul, who died from a
brain abscess only twenty months after the boy's birth. Yet he is
certain that it is from his father that he received his literary gifts,
for at the *collège* of Toulenne, near Langon, Jean-Paul won all
the school prizes. But since he was the eldest son, his father took
him out of school before he could obtain his baccalaureate degree, in order that he might enter the family business of import-
ing barrel wood from Austria. When the grandfather liquidated
his business in 1870 and retired to his property near Langon,
Jean-Paul was left without a job or a diploma; at the time of his
death he was employed in a bank. Jean-Paul was more interested
in literature than in business, however, and even wrote poetry on
occasion. He left his family beautiful editions, notably of Montaigne and of La Bruyère. Early in life he had lost his religious
faith, and François later found some pathetic letters from the
priests who had loved him. "He reacted violently against religion
as it was manifested in his wife's family and in political life after
1870." [4] Mauriac has often speculated how his own life might
have been altered if, instead of this irreligious father, it had been
his pious Jansenist mother whom he had lost at this early age.

Though he apparently never knew his mother's father, a Bordeaux merchant, Mauriac remembers clearly his paternal grandfather who died in 1890, in the vast home at Langon which later
served as the setting for his novel *Genitrix*. Mauriac recalls that
this grandfather used to bring them *foie gras* or other delicacies
from Langon and that, on his last visit, the day before his death
he looked through the albums containing photographs of de-
ceased relatives, sighing "what a cemetery." On the following day
he returned, went to visit all the places he loved—his property of
Malagar and the hospice of Langon he administered—and after
dinner repaired to the home of an elderly lady friend with whom
he played bridge every evening.

It is here that the supernatural intervenes. His elderly friend asked him if he would like to accompany her to church for the Benediction. My grandfather had been very anti-clerical all his life, sworn adversary of the Marist Fathers of Verdelais. Although he had softened somewhat (under the influence of my mother whom he adored) he had not set foot in a church for many years. Now, to the surprise of everyone, he agreed to accompany the old lady and appeared very reflective until the end of the service. On his return on the road . . . he fell down, helpless. They carried him to his bed. To his friend who begged him to pray he had time to answer 'We are saved by faith' joining his hands together.[5]

This incident seems to have influenced Mauriac deeply, for we find it reproduced in his novel *Genitrix*. In *Les Maisons fugitives,* Mauriac adds, to illustrate his grandfather's passionate love for his native soil, that he had insisted on having some of the earth from his Malagar estate brought to cover his tomb: "He brought back over his corpse, as a blanket, this beloved clay."

The only male survivor of his grandfather's family was Mauriac's uncle Louis. As younger son he had had the right to continue his studies and had become a lawyer. On his brother's death he was made guardian for the five children, came twice a month to administer their estate, and during his lifetime as an old bachelor gave the children the greater part of his own fortune. He will appear as the uncle Xavier in Mauriac's later *Le Mystère Frontenac* in which every detail of his life is true, Mauriac assured me, even including his mistress and his terrible death. Like his brother Jean-Paul he was an atheist or at least an agnostic—he never attended church—and when the children returned from mass they would find him still in bed or in his carpet slippers, smoking caporal cigarettes; Mauriac's mother, who felt great esteem but little love for him, worried about his influence on the children.[6]

But the greatest factor in Mauriac's childhood was the dominance of women in his upbringing. "It is not without reason that I was to become the novelist of Genitrix. Around me, when I was a child, women reigned."[7] After his father's death the family moved to the third floor in the home of his grandmother, who occupied the first two. This elderly dame, for all her piety and tenderness toward her descendants, was conscious of her dignity as head of the family, and Mauriac recalls hearing her close abruptly a family discussion with the ejaculation: "Who is the mistress here?" [8] Like an old queen this aged grandmother held sway over her three daughters, her two sons-in-law, her estates, and her dwellings, mourning constantly the death of a beloved son whose mysterious fate was always kept a secret by François' mother and aunts. She was constantly attended by a nun and was visited often by priests who venerated her almost as a saint. Indeed she had received permission to have religious services celebrated in her own chapel, in her suburban home of Château-Lange some seven kilometers from Bordeaux on the road toward Spain. (This Château under the name of Ousillane plays an important role in the setting of Mauriac's early novel, *La Robe prétexte*, and it was on the streetcar which went to Château-Lange through Talence that Raymond in *Le Désert de l'amour* fell in love with Maria Cross.) The employees of the tram called Château-Lange "the house of the priests" because whenever there was a cassock on board it always got off at this house. [9]

Because the refinery of her parents had fallen on evil days, this grandmother "of a good family" had married a wealthy Bordeaux merchant, "a self-made man." Extremely ugly in her old age, she would press little François tenderly in her arms, calling him a rascal: " 'All men are rascals.' Probably an allusion to the infidelities of a husband, obliged to travel frequently in his commerce of tissues and shawls." [10] Even as a child Mauriac recalls being troubled by the unyielding bigotry of the pious women of the household, their absolute conviction that there was "no salvation outside the church." [11] When the priest at his grandmother's deathbed pronounced a funeral oration on the theme "She was a great soul," little Mauriac had difficulty in reconciling this description with the stern, dominating figure of the old lady he had known. [12]

But it is the enveloping personality of his mother which stands out above all others in Mauriac's early development, who occupies a privileged place in his autobiography *Commencements d'une vie* and in all his reminiscences, and who is idolized as the central figure in *Le Mystère Frontenac*. "Everything which touched her took on in my eyes a sacred character, and shared in her perfection, even servants and objects." [13] Though she probably had never read a Jansenist tract, Mauriac assured me, his mother in her simple austerity was really a Jansenist at heart, and her children were brought up in strict observance of all the religious ceremonies of the calendar.

Life was concentrated in the maternal room, which was hung with gray around a Chinese lamp covered with a pink *cannelé* shade. On the mantelpiece Chapu's Joan of Arc listened to her voices. According to the seasons, the cries of martins rent the stifling air of evening or the deep boom of the cathedral filled the Christmas night, or the sirens of vessels whined in the fog.[14] At nine o'clock his mother would kneel for prayer, with her little brood pressed closely about her. "We knew that the Infinite Being demands of children that they sleep hands crossed on their breast, palms as if nailed to our bodies, clutching the blessed medals and the scapulary of Mount Carmel which must not be removed even for baths." [15] After kissing each of the five children the mother would go down to the grandmother's apartment, and little François recalled the terrible resounding noise of the door closing behind her, leaving him only the refuge of sleep against this solitude. Yet if Mauriac's memories of childhood were full of loneliness and sadness, he is careful to point out that this was not due to religion—for this gave him more joys than sorrows.

II *School Days*

When François was five years old his mother took him to the kindergarten of Sister Adrienne, opposite the Sainte Marie school of the Marianites which his older brothers attended. He felt himself always in disgrace because of a torn eyelid which had given him the nickname of *Coco-bel-oeil* and contributed to his frail and unprepossessing appearance. His brother Raymond, writing under his nom de plume of Housilane, tells us that this accident occurred when François, at the age of three, was striking his little wooden horse with a stick.[16] Mauriac's own version is a little different. "It must have been in 1889 (I was four years old) that the end of a whip, which one of my brothers was trying to tear from my hands and released suddenly, struck my eye which an iron wire penetrated. Our maid Octavie, terrified, pulled on the whip and the eyelid followed. It had to be sewed on. I remember the coachman who held me, the howls I uttered, the terror I felt at each visit from Dr. Dulac." [17] This accident, however minor in

appearance, seems to have been partly responsible for the lad's
inferiority complex, and perhaps may have entered into his portrait of the pitiful, bashful hero of *Le Baiser au lépreux.*

In 1892 when François was seven he moved across the street to
the Marianite school. This seventh year and those immediately
following were perhaps the most unhappy of his childhood.
"Everything wounded me: terror of the masters, anguish because
of lessons badly learned, compositions, examinations; incapacity
of living far from what I loved, separated, if only for a day, from
my mother." [18] It was here that occurred "the crime of his seventh
year" which he could still remember seventy years later. Desperate at always being last even in reading (though he felt that he
could read better than the others), trying to erase the grade on his
report card he had moistened his handkerchief and rubbed until
he made a hole in the paper. This was an act so grave, his mother
pointed out to him, that it could put grownups in prison.[19] Such
fear of his teachers and comrades did little François feel at this
time that he would shut himself up in a latrine during the whole
period of recess. His only joy came at the approach of evening
"which brought me back to that Chinese lamp, to the evening
meal, to the reading of *Saint Nicolas* by the fireside, to the prayer
recited in common." [20] But the following morning he would
awake in the icy room lighted by a candle or lamp, the chilblains
on his hands and feet being no excuse for missing class. The obsession for the warm family circle around the lamp seems to have
remained with Mauriac throughout his life, for he recently wrote
that all his life he had tried to rebuild this nest, the shelter of his
childhood—even in war days in a village room or in a camp near
the front.[21]

The year 1896 was the memorable date of his first communion,
followed two years later, at the age of ten, by his entrance in the
Collège des Marianites then being built in the suburb of Caudé-
ran. Mauriac's memories of this college seem to be mixed, for he
once wrote that the promiscuity of the college made him suffer
and seek solitude, his favorite recreation being roller skating because he could do this without any companion.[22] Yet almost seventy years later he could write: "I was happy and loved at Grand
Lebrun." [23]

At five-thirty every morning the servant would awaken
François. After a rapid toilet—for in this icy room it would have

taken heroism to wash—and a few swallows of hot chocolate the boys would await at the door the arrival of the "parcours," as the wheezy old school bus was called. Then François would have a half hour to drowse, the hood of his light coat pulled down over his head like a monk's cowl. "Heart-breaking dawns, somber city, thirst for escape. It is then that a child's heart, a frozen heart, is accustomed to seek God. . . . The trees of Grand Lebrun were outlined on the sky. The enormous building, all lighted up, resembled a steamer." [24] What a long and arduous day these youngsters had to endure. Half an hour to study, a short recess followed by two hours of classes; another quarter hour to play, then study hall till noon. Then work began again at one-thirty, lasting, except for a half hour for tea, until six-thirty. It is true that the last hour or two of study hall pleased the lad, not only because it betokened release but because he employed it not on his lessons but rather to write in his journal or to compose poetry. Sometimes, on various pretexts, François would obtain permission to go outside to absorb under the great trees the breath of oncoming night in the mist. "Doubtless I lived then in a perpetual state of poetic trance, there was nothing in my poor life I did not wish to transfigure." [25] This was the time when poets began to surround him and serve him. "I interposed between reality and myself all the lyricism of the last century. Lamartine, Musset and Vigny were the first to enter my life and among the moderns I succeeded in finding sublime beauties even in Sully-Prudhomme and in Samain. Verlaine, Rimbaud, Baudelaire and Jammes came up only after I had finished college." [26]

With one exception Mauriac does not show himself very tender in his recollections of teachers at Grand Lebrun. These he divides into three groups; at the bottom of the scale the lay members brought in from the outside. Above them he places the friars who performed the function of monitors, clad in frock coats, with astonishing silk hats on their heads, shod with felt slippers which kept them warm and allowed them to walk with wolflike steps to surprise the unwary. "With nothing to do but spy on us in the long evening study hall, they had placed screens in front of the lamps which reflected the light on us. They excelled in creating, in the glasses of their spectacles, reflections which made it impossible for us to observe the direction of their glance." [27] And just when they thought one of them to be immersed in his favorite book, his ter-

rible voice would cry out: "Mauriac, bring me the note that Lacaze has just passed to you." They had enormous noses, rendered
soft and black, Mauriac tells us, by the use of snuff. The boys
feared their justice because it was so mysterious, apparently without any regard to the gravity of the offense.

At the top of the hierarchy young Mauriac placed the priests.
One in particular stood out above all the rest, l'abbé Péquignot,
professor of rhetoric, whose prestige was immense. "The worst
roughhouser among us would not have dared raise his nose in
front of him. His courses seemed to us sublime. It was he who
awakened our intelligence, gave us a taste for ideas, made the
authors on the program come alive." [28] Mauriac lamented thirty
years later that Grand Lebrun did not reciprocate his love and
would never invite him to preside on Honors Day, as did the
lycées of Giraudoux and the Tharaud brothers.[29] He was wrong,
for half a century after graduation he did receive this mark of
appreciation. In his speech at Grand Lebrun on this occasion,
Mauriac recalled the difficulty he had always experienced with
figures, equations, and formulas, before delivering an eloquent
tribute to his former teacher, l'abbé Péquignot. "It was of you that
one could say, so little incarnate were you, that you had a body
only because you had no means of doing otherwise. You accomplished a miracle, in the midst of preparation for the bachot, to
make me love Pascal and Racine. You are responsible for making
me the novelist I have become—perhaps it has cost you extra time
in purgatory." [30] My own visit some years ago with the courteous
Marist Fathers of Grand Lebrun impressed me with the love and
admiration they feel for this, their most distinguished alumnus.

III Summer Vacations

Mauriac recalls the exhilaration he experienced in the religious
festivals at Grand Lebrun, particularly that of Corpus Christi day
with its chorus of three hundred children, the incense of its perfume burners, the banners held at an angle to avoid the low
branches of the trees. But his greatest joy came when he saw the
workers laying planks under the trees for the distribution of
prizes: this presaged for him the treasure of vacation time in the
countryside soon to follow.

Until he became eighteen Mauriac and his family spent their

summers on the ancestral estates in the Landes among the pine trees, the sand and the cicadas of Saint-Symphorien.

Thus entered into me, for all eternity, those implacable summers, that forest crawling with cicadas under a brazen sky darkened at times by the immense sulfurous veil of conflagrations. However burning the afternoon, the brook called La Hure and the floating fogs and marshy meadows it drags after it gave forth in the evening a dangerous chill. . . . This breath of mint, of moist grass and water, mingled with all that was abandoned to night by the moor freed from sunlight, furnace suddenly grown cool: perfume of burned heather, warm sand and resin—delightful fragrance of this country covered with ashes, studded with trees with open flanks.[31]

It was autumn that François loved best, when in the midst of glowing foliage he would sit on a pine trunk, half-melancholy at the thought of vacation's end, half-joyous at the prospect of rejoining Bordeaux which never seemed more beautiful to him than in the transfiguration lent by absence.

After he became eighteen it was an entirely different aspect of the country he came to love—the arbors and terrace of Malagar with its vast sweep across the Garonne to Langon and to the vineyards of Château Yquem far in the distance. Later it was this second aspect which Mauriac preferred, this Malagar to which he still returns every Easter and summer, whose charm consists for him in its double role—the confluence of former days with the recent past and present. These two different landscapes reappear constantly in all Mauriac's novels. "From this countryside I have never emerged, nor have my works, and that is probably why those who have loved me praise me,—a weakness however in the eyes of others." [32]

IV *Bordeaux—Triumphs and Disappointments*

In 1901-2 Mauriac studied rhetoric with his beloved master l'abbé Péquignot, received first prize for his essay in philosophy, passed the first part of his *bachot*, but was failed twice the following year in philosophy. Ashamed to return to Grand Lebrun, François spent the next year in the *lycée*, where he had as professor the brother-in-law of André Gide, and finally passed his examination. Terrified by Mauriac's attack of pleurisy, his family decided that François must avoid fatigue and take two years for his *licence* degree in letters at the University of Bordeaux. In 1904 he was a student of Fortunat Strowski (later a famous professor at the Sorbonne and literary critic) whom he liked because he was a specialist in Pascal and even more because he dared read to his class a poem of Francis Jammes. In 1905 he had as professor the famous André LeBreton and passed his *licence* degree. The subject for his dissertation was as follows: "The thought of death deceives us for it makes us forget to live." Taking the negative, thanks to his knowledge of Pascal he obtained a grade of 18 out of 20, but received a zero in Greek on the oral, which he made up in October. The next year he wasted, working on a thesis in Bordeaux on the subject "the origins of franciscanism in France," then decided to go to Paris to prepare for L'Ecole des Chartes.

The last three years in Bordeaux seem to have left a rather bitter taste in Mauriac's recollection, though he did have two close friends, André Lacaze and Xavier Darbon, became acquainted with contemporary poetry, especially that of Francis Jammes, and met Alexis Léger (St.-John Perse), future Nobel laureate. Though he read Anatole France, Paul Bourget, Pierre Loti, and Claudel, the master he preferred was Barrès.[33]

The section entitled *Bordeaux*, added to *Commencements d'une vie* of his *Ecrits intimes*, testifies to the importance which this city, at the same time so beautiful and so depressing, was to occupy in his future works. "The history of Bordeaux is the history of my body and of my soul. . . . Bordeaux is my childhood and my adolescence detached from me, petrified. . . . Up to my twentieth year my destiny was comprised in this city and its countryside: it never overlapped its contours. A Chinese wall separated Guyenne for us from the rest of the universe." [34] And just as this Chinese wall separated him geographically from the world outside, so did Catholicism bound another world, beyond which he would have felt himself lost and adrift.

Though his maternal grandparents had been sugar refiners and cloth merchants in Bordeaux, they were strangers to the proud Anglo-Saxon race of wine merchants and shipowners whose haughty aristocracy Mauriac was to satirize so bitterly in his early novel *Préséances*. On the paternal side, his grandparents, as we have seen, were landowners, and Mauriac feels that it is perhaps this rustic heredity which explains the restlessness from which he suffered in Bordeaux—and indeed later in Paris also.[35] At any rate, in this city of stone, Mauriac felt a desire to escape from this confining atmosphere of convention and conservatism. "The tragic atmosphere of Bordeaux for me lies in this drama which I lived there: a prodigious individual life repressed, without any possibility for expression or overflow." [36]

Mauriac confesses frankly, however, that wherever he goes, it is this Bordeaux and its surroundings that he has taken with him. This explains why all the settings of his successful works are in his native region, rather than in the Paris where his later life has been spent.

However much we may play the Parisian, rejoice at living in Paris, Bordeaux is well aware that when it is necessary to descend into ourself as novelist, to seek landscapes and characters, it is not the Champs Elysées or the Boulevards that we find there, nor our comrades and friends from the banks of the Seine—but the family estates, the monotonous vines, the lusterless moors, the most somber suburbs seen through the misty panes of the college bus—and our characters are born . . . resembling my country grandparents, my cousins of the moor, all that provincial fauna I used to spy on as a frail child.[37]

But this spiritual city in which all ugliness has been erased or changed to poetry until it has become a work of art still brings suffering to the author when he confronts it with the actual Bordeaux he revisits, the dark city of mud and stone. "My province has made of me a mule with blinded eyes to grind its grain." [38] And Mauriac concludes with an apology for all his offenses against this city of his birth which has filled his memory with grotesque and charming faces, landscapes, impressions and emotions, everything necessary for his writing, and which has pardoned him for his cruel strictures.[39] Indeed it was in 1939 on the triumphant performance of his play *Asmodée* in Bordeaux that the final reconciliation between Mauriac and his native city took place.

V   *Paris and the Meeting with Barrès*

Mauriac reached Paris in September, 1906. His decision to prepare for entrance in the Ecole des Chartes had been reached not from any overriding interest in history but chiefly because this was the only one of the Grandes Ecoles which did not require mathematics for admission. After failing on his first entrance examination he was finally accepted in November, 1908. Some years before, in Bordeaux, Mauriac had joined the progressive and democratic Catholic movement of Marc Sangnier, known as Le Sillon (to be described at length in his first novel *L'Enfant chargé de chaînes*) and, thanks to the victory of this group over L'Action française among the Paris students, Mauriac was elected President of the Catholic student union. Six months after his entrance in the Ecole des Chartes he resigned in order to devote himself entirely to literature. What decided him was a meeting with Charles-Francis Caillard, Director of the review *Le Temps Présent*, who, an admirer of Mauriac's poems, asked him to collaborate as poetry editor of the review, and offered to publish his first slender volume of verse for the sum of 500 francs. The book appeared in November, 1909 under the title *Les Mains jointes* (Joined Hands) which had been suggested by Mauriac's friend, Jean de la Ville Mirmont.

In his essay *La Rencontre avec Barrès*, later republished in *Ecrits intimes* along with *Commencements, Journal d'un homme de 30 ans* and *Du Côté de chez Proust*, Mauriac relates at some length the miraculous reception of his first work by the great Barrès. On the morning of February 8, 1910, Mauriac received from the hands of his landlady an envelope stamped from the Chamber of Deputies, which read as follows:

You are a great poet whom I admire, a true poet, measured, tender and profound, who does not try to force his voice, of a nature to move us in regard to our childhood. I should like to say this to the public. That is why I have delayed in thanking you for this precious little book, which I have read and reread during the past fortnight. I am profoundly happy that we have a poet.

MAURICE BARRÈS[40]

Then Mauriac remembered having received from a bookseller, when he was home with the grippe in Bordeaux during the New Year's holidays, a request from Maurice Barrès for the book. Such had been his awe and admiration for Barrès, whose *culte du moi* had been the great influence on his last three years in Bordeaux, that he had not dared earlier to send Barrès a copy, feeling it unworthy of the master. After his letter of thanks to Barrès he received from the latter another letter, explaining that he had mentioned the volume in an article for *l'Echo de Paris* and would later give it an entire review. Indeed two days later the first article appeared, praising *Les Mains jointes* "precious poem, tender and devout." [41]

Thrilled by this recognition from the writer he worshiped, Mauriac went to a lecture Barrès gave on his *Voyage de Sparte*, introduced himself with emotion and noticed the master's astonishment. "What," said Barrès, "you're not a little seminary student. It's true," he added, "some of your poems are very passionate." Then he invited young Mauriac to walk with him to the Chamber of Deputies. This first meeting, however, was somewhat disillusioning, for Barrès proceeded to demolish many of Mauriac's early gods—Francis Jammes, Claudel, even Bourget.

On March 21, 1910, the promised review by Barrès appeared in the *Echo de Paris*. After telling how he had run across *Les Mains jointes* on a visit to Bourget, Barrès stated that he was struck in this book by:

A charming gift of spirituality, joined to youthfulness and pure taste. . . . It is the poetry of a child of happy family, the poem of the little boy well-behaved, delicate, well brought up, whose light nothing has tarnished, over-sensitive, with a mad note of voluptuousness.

Comparing the young poet to Verlaine minus the remorse, to a Sainte-Beuve less inclined to physiology, Barrès finds that everything here is tender, vague, dreamy, and full of the warmth of the nest, before concluding:

Young François Mauriac, in this volume in which I do not find a single stupidity (truly prodigious for a poet) gives an excellent definition of himself: he speaks to us of his past "of a mystical and reasonable child." I confirm his diagnostic: he has reasonableness and even good sense. This is a guarantee for his salvation, let him attach himself solidly to this share of good sense so that his poetic genius, whose April I am happy to salute, may give us its four seasons of flowers and fruits.[42]

Mauriac was to learn much later that Barrès, in writing this eulogy, was moved in large measure by the emotion he still felt at the recent tragic death of his nephew, Charles Demange. Apparently Barrès showed little interest in Mauriac's later development,

for in one of their later meetings in 1922 shortly before the death
of Barrès he asked Mauriac what he was doing. When Mauriac
answered in surprise "Haven't you received *Le Baiser au
lépreux?*" the vague gesture of Barrès indicated clearly enough
that he had not read this work, the first of his books for which
Mauriac did not blush.[43] Nevertheless, this early recognition of
young Mauriac by the great master was the turning point in his
career. It brought him to the attention of critics (Emile Faguet),
gained for him a group of new friends such as Valléry-Radot,
François LeGrix and the poet André Lafon, and opened several
salons to him, among them that of Mme Alphonse Daudet where
he came to know León Daudet, Jean Cocteau, and later Marcel
Proust.[44] Above all, it confirmed his decision to devote himself to
literature. As he wrote many years later at the age of fifty:

Merely, from the very outset, having on the credit side enough money
to work without worries, an honorable family, a province, memories
of childhood, a religious sensitivity fortified by an inhuman repression,
the favor of the Muses and the gift for writing, I let myself be carried
along. An instinct doubtless informed me that I could live according
to my own heart . . . and that all the rest would come of itself,
would be added unto me. At the article by Barrès saluting my *Mains
jointes* I recognized the starting whistle of the train official; I was on
the track with the stations ahead clearly foreseen.[45]

It is interesting to compare this prophetic discovery of the young
Mauriac by Barrès with the similar prescience shown by André
Gide in the cases of Saint-Exupéry and Jean Giono.

VI   *Marital and Martial Experience*

In 1911 Mauriac was working on a second volume of poetry,
Adieu à l'adolescence and his first novel *L'Enfant chargé de
chaînes.* The latter, published in the magazine *Mercure de
France,* was rejected both by the Editions du Mercure and by
Stock, but appeared in 1913 under the imprint of Grasset. This
year (1911) was marked also by an unhappy love affair and by a
pilgrimage with André Lafon to the home of Francis Jammes at
Orthez in the Basque country.[46] In 1912 he became acquainted
with Jeanne Lafont whom he married June 3, 1913, after having
been at first refused by her father, a banker who took a dim view
of this budding poet. When he asked his prospective son-in-law

sarcastically if he expected to belong some day to the French Academy, Mauriac answered rather brashly that since there had to be forty "immortals" each generation it was unthinkable that he could escape this honor. Apparently "this terrible man" was amused rather than offended by the reply. (Mauriac confesses that he took several traits of his father-in-law for the protagonists of *Genitrix* and *Le Noeud de Vipères*.)[47]

April of 1914 witnessed the birth of his first son, Claude, and of his second novel *La Robe prétexte*. When World War I broke out in June, Mauriac was rejected by the army for physical disability but like Cocteau joined the Sanitary Service at the Front. At his request he was later sent to Salonika, but soon after his arrival contracted a fever and finally had to be repatriated and was demobilized in 1918. On his recovery, he completed by 1920 a novel *La Chair et le sang* begun in 1914, and followed this in 1921 with his fourth novel, *Préséances*. Then in 1922 came his first great success with *Le Baiser au lépreux*, his first book to exceed the restricted sale of three thousand copies and reach a broad public. At the age of thirty-seven, Mauriac had suddenly achieved fame, and the period of his mature productivity had begun.

CHAPTER 2

Early Autobiographical Novels

BEFORE the dawn of Mauriac's literary reputation "came up like thunder" with *Le Baiser au lépreux,* he had already completed four apprentice novels and as early as 1921 was working on a fifth, *Le Mal.* Different in tone and setting as these may be, they nevertheless share in common one characteristic which sets them apart from his later work, except for his *Mystère Frontenac.* This is their autobiographical quality. Their interest for us today lies primarily in their revelation of the deep conflict underlying Mauriac's adolescence: the dichotomy between his deeply religious environment on the one hand, his growing sensuality and awakening to the joys of nature on the other.

I L'Enfant chargé de chaînes (*1913*)

L'Enfant chargé de chaînes (Young Man in Chains), written between 1909 and 1912 and not translated into English until a half century after publication, attracted little attention from the critics or the general public. One of the most subjective of Mauriac's novels, it portrays the alternating enthusiasm and disillusionment of its youthful hero, Jean-Paul, torn from his apathy by a momentary desire to lose himself in the social crusade of the young Catholic movement called "Faith and Love." Relapsing into discouragement from which he makes a brief effort to escape through sensual pleasure, he is rescued at last by the pure devotion of his gentle cousin, Marthe.

Awkward and groping in technique, barren of incident and cluttered up with moralizing and mawkish despair, conventional and unconvincing in its depiction of the flesh pots of Paris, this first novel nevertheless shows flashes of poetic charm when the author reverts to the atmosphere of damp woods and marshland in his native Landes near Bordeaux. The student of Mauriac is interested moreover in the faithful reflection of the author through the central character, the young man weighed down with chains of skepticism and sensuality. The portrait of Jean-Paul is not a pretty one, and perhaps the author has been unduly harsh in his self-condemnation. As François LeGrix put it, Jean-Paul is "always a sinner but without the energy to sin very much, pure in spite of himself, obsessed by the nostalgia of the faults he doesn't commit because they do not tempt him enough, and yet incapable of being satisfied with such relative innocence." [1] His egotism is apparent in the fact that he feels no pity for Marthe in her apparently hopeless love for him. "Ah, little girl, how I envy you for loving me."

Yet if we make allowance for the exaggeration with which Mauriac has painted this self-portrait, we may find in Jean-Paul an almost literal reproduction of the author's own youth. He too was a Sorbonne student, publishing verses in obscure reviews, enamored of the same poets—Baudelaire, Verlaine, Francis Jammes—seeking mystic satisfaction in spiritual retreats, anxious to give himself with devotion to Christian democracy in the Sillon movement. Disillusioned with this venture, Mauriac puts in the mouth of his hero these revealing words: "I was always an amateur of souls. . . . This or that soul to whose interests I thought I was devoting all my efforts did nothing more than add an item to my collection." With what amazing lucidity Mauriac here lays bare the preoccupation which was to mark all his work as a novelist: "Some of us are born with a restless wish to do good to our brothers—others with a taste for the delicious pleasure which comes from probing into the intricacies of human souls."

II   La Robe prétexte (*1914*)

La Robe prétexte, published in 1914, covers the adolescence of Mauriac preceding his move to Paris and the experiences described in his first novel. An explanation of the title is found in the book itself. "As a young Roman, having attained the age of manhood, put aside the *robe prétexte* (*praetexta*), the white robe with trimming of royal purple which was the insignia of adolescence—thus . . . I said farewell to my sixteenth year."

Whereas *L'Enfant chargé de chaînes* showed the influence of Barrès in its cynical, detached style, *La Robe prétexte* is warm, discursive, mellow and poetic, impregnated with gentle humor. It affords a much more sympathetic portrait of its hero, who of

course is young Mauriac himself. The inventive power of the
novelist is beginning to show itself, particularly in the creation of
the legendary father who, like Gauguin, had wandered off to the
tropics to paint immortal landscapes. Yet the feminine protagonist, the hero's cousin Camille, is as shadowy and unsubstantial a
creation as the Marthe of the earlier novel, and the technique of
composition is as awkward and formless as that of its predecessor.

Mauriac has not yet succeeded in freeing himself from his
purely subjective impressions, rendered here almost in the rambling context of a journal. The portrait of his grandmother is also
that of his own mother whose ascetic Jansenist attitude shielded
the young lad from the temptations of the world. The loving portrait of l'abbé Maysonnave who introduced the boy to Pascal was
inspired by Mauriac's favorite professor, l'abbé Péquignot, in the
Marianite *collège*. The description of the religious ceremonies at
the college and of the Corpus Christi procession which affected
the youngster so deeply are duplicated almost word for word in
the later autobiographical *Commencements d'une vie*, as well as
the poetic depiction of Ousillane (Château-Lange), the country
home of his grandmother near Bordeaux.

For the first time we may glimpse here Mauriac's penchant for
satirical observation, not yet scathing as in the later *Préséances*,
but rather mildly quizzical. Introduced by his aunt to social in-
equalities, Jacques learned early that it was contemptible to devote oneself to any other commerce than that of wine. "But even
there I learned to observe different gradations; those who sold
superior wine took precedence over those who also sold ordinary
wine—and those who sold only ordinary wine merited scarcely
any more consideration than a doctor or a mere professor at the
university." Equally amusing is the portrait of their poor relation,
the old maid Mlle Dumoliers. Ever fearful of potential masculine
advances which would imperil her virtue, she had hung a man's
stovepipe hat in her vestibule to frighten away overzealous
gallants.

Yet our main concern in this early novel is with the central protagonist, Jacques, who reflects so accurately Mauriac's own adolescence. A mysterious temptation drew the lad away from the hum-
drum life of the inner city to the busy port where he found himself
in a different universe. Here he felt a nostalgia for travel, facing
"this black water in which the image of pontoons trembled upside-

down." We may note the struggle which went on in the youth's breast between the emotional joys of his Catholic ambiance and his awakening sensuality toward the female sex. "In college I was one of those scrupulous and devout children whom the ignorance of evil delivers from evil. As an adolescent I did not think there was any higher ambition than to avoid all impurities and pass over the world like a great archangel." Alas, when his family sends him off to Paris to break up a clandestine love affair with his cousin Camille, our young hero is about to fall into the clutches of a demimondaine. Providentially he is saved at the last moment by a dispatch from Bordeaux, announcing the fatal illness of his grandmother. "One of my relatives, the most beloved one, decided to die and dig her tomb to separate voluptuousness from my desire." Rather a drastic remedy, the reader may object, to save so fragile a virtue.

It may well be that Amélie Fillon is unduly eulogistic when she calls *La Robe prétexte* an enchantment, comparing it to Colette's *La Maison de Claudine* for its "impression of naturalness, of cheerful youth, of cruel observation expressed with so much good humor." [2] Loosely composed and slow-moving, it is still an apprentice work, but not without charm for its perceptive revelation of the author's own adolescence.

III   La Chair et le sang (*1920*)

La Chair et le sang (Flesh and Blood) marks a decisive step in Mauriac's development as a novelist. Here for the first time we find not merely the purely subjective reflections of his own youth but a novel of passion, with varied and complex characters, dramatic and almost melodramatic plot, and admirable richness of poetic description. Here the themes treated are significant and diverse: comparison between the Catholic and Protestant philosophies of life, satire of bourgeois smugness and provincialism, contrast of the feverish, hothouse environment of Parisian artists and poetasters with the healthy simplicity of rural existence. In addition, we have the motif already adumbrated in the earlier novels, and which will become the hallmark, so to speak, of Mauriac's entire production, namely, the conflict between the sensual appetites of man—the flesh and blood of the title—and the desperate craving for purity and sanctity.

The first part of *La Chair et le sang* is vastly superior to the

second. A young peasant, Claude Favereau, has just abandoned
the seminary to return to the country estate where his father is
manager. At the same time the new owner, M. Dupont-Gunther,
a coarse and cynical businessman, arrives with his two children:
Edouard, blasé, ironic, and disillusioned; May, aristocratic, cul-
tured, and sophisticated but with a vein of sensuality just below
the surface. Along with them appear the fantastic, Machiavellian
governess, Mme Gonzalès, former mistress and procuress of M.
Dupont-Gunther, and her daughter Edith, groomed by her mother
for an attempt to ensnare the sexagenarian proprietor into the
trap of matrimony. Both Edouard and May become fascinated
with Claude, who unites intelligence and Catholic fervor with his
robust peasant charm. Edouard falls temporarily under the spell
of Edith's amorous advances and departs with her for Paris. May,
despite her patrician reserve, allows herself to be kissed by the
young peasant and then, blackmailed by the spying Mme Gonzalès, agrees to accept her father's plan and marry a solid, rather
stupid scion of bourgeois respectability, Marcel Castagnède.

In the second part we learn that May, disgusted with her
brother's desertion, seems to have become satisfied and even
happy in her conversion to Catholicism, absorption in the bourgeois tedium of the Castagnède family, and enjoyment of the
physical pleasures of matrimony. Edouard, however, after a brief
period in which Edith has goaded him to attempt success as an
artist, becomes so thoroughly satiated with the futility of social
pretensions in Paris that he takes refuge in a shabby hotel in
Châlons with the morbid decision to commit suicide in five days
unless either Edith or Claude responds to his despairing letters.
Though Mauriac keeps the reader in suspense during the various
occurences which prevent either from arriving in time, there is
something artificial and contrived in these events which renders
the denouement theatrical and melodramatic.

It is not difficult to note in this novel the author's increased
capacity for character creation. The wily and scheming Mme
Gonzalès, the brutal and profligate M. Dupont-Gunther, are, it is
true, picturesque caricatures rather than deeply analyzed personages. Yet Edouard, until his somewhat unconvincing deterioration
at the end, is a rather original depiction of the would-be esthete,
capricious, bored with existence, conscious of his own incapacity
either to create or to love. May, the puritanical Huguenot who

feels guilty even in her connubial joys, the cruel and perverse girl
who can stir young Favereau with passion yet feel no qualm of
conscience for his suffering at the announcement of her marriage,
is a less shadowy figure than her predecessors Marthe and Camille. The most convincing character, however, is Claude Favereau, probably because he is the most subjective, the closest to
Mauriac himself, a true brother of the earlier Jean-Paul and
Jacques. As with most of Mauriac's heroes, we find in him a
poignant conflict between his ardent, sensual nature and his anguished striving for purity.

Yet the chief attraction which this early novel may still hold
for the reader comes from its exquisite descriptions of nature,
scarcely to be excelled in his later works. The novel was written
at Mauriac's country estate of Malagar, and its rustic setting of
vineyards and orchards, overlooking the broad sweep of the
Garonne, is fragrant and appealing. Michael Maloney has perhaps
pointed out better than any other critic the intricate subtlety with
which Mauriac has combined these descriptions of nature with
the events they accompany and in part produce: the inception
of Claude's and May's infatuation, for instance, during the sultry
heat of July, the black wintry rain which envelops Claude as a
prison when he learns of May's desertion, the voluptuous and
perfumed awakening of the earth in springtime, rendering
Claude's suffering more poignant when May returns to the estate
as the bride of another.[3]

IV Préséances (1921)

Préséances (Precedences) marks little advance over its predecessors except in the domain of social satire. As in the case of
Daudet's Tartarin novels, this mordant caricature of the great
wine merchants of Bordeaux brought Mauriac little affection from
his fellow citizens. Like *La Chair et le sang* the first half of this
novel, devoted almost entirely to social satire, is incomparably
better than the second. Edmond Jaloux finds this indeed "an admirable painting of vanity, as harsh, as exact as certain tableaux
of Thackeray." [4] In the college these sons of the great wine merchants form a sort of closed corporation, an aristocracy looking
down with scorn on poorer but more intelligent students. In the
society of the town their snobbery is shown by the fact that they
marry only among themselves and all bear English names—James,

John, Percy, Bertie, Harry, and Willy. Their exclusive club is called "London and Westminster." What characterizes these haughty patricians above all is monotonous conformity. "The Sons of the Great Houses are, so to speak, interchangeable, all impeccable (fitted out by the same tailor), all sportsmen leaving the office at five o'clock, all of them exempt from the common laws of civility, capable of bowing or not bowing, incorruptible dispensers of disdain."

While the plot in the first part of the novel does not put too much strain on the reader's credulity, the second part, like that of *La Chair et le sang*, is a medley of fantastic melodrama. It may be, as Amélie Fillon suggests that "with this mixture of mysticism, idealism, adventure and satire," Mauriac has attempted to join the Slavic with the Latin genius.[5] The character of Florence resembles in its heartlessness and violent sensuality that of May in the preceding volume. We may see in her an early incarnation of an idea to be found so often in Mauriac's later work; namely, that woman in her role of Delilah personifies the sin of lust, man's greatest obstacle on the path of salvation.

Though *Préséances* like *La Robe prétexte* is written in the first person, we find few subjective indications in this narrator, other than his reminiscences of the college and one curious reference to the religious superstitions of Mauriac's own childhood. "I crossed the vestibule with white and black tiles (where I used to walk only on the white ones because the slightest false step would have signified that I was not in a state of grace)." More closely akin to the heroes of the three earlier volumes and to the youthful Mauriac himself is the attractive and romantic Rimbaud-like figure of his friend Augustin, so studious, solitary, and contemptuous of worldly conformity, in whom blazed an almost mystic passion for idealism and purity.

V   Le Mal (1924)

To these four novels published before 1922 we should add a fifth one, *Le Mal* (The Enemy), since it was composed between 1921 and 1923, and since it, too, is an autobiographical novel, at least in regard to the hero's childhood. After it appeared in 1924 in the magazine *Demain,* Mauriac refused to allow it to be published in book form until it came out in a semi-deluxe limited edition some eleven years later. On that occasion an anonymous reviewer sardonically quoted a remark Giroudoux had once uttered: "When we have made a failure of something, we can always publish it in a deluxe edition for the great satisfaction of book collectors."

Hourdin found the hero of *Le Mal*, Fabien Dézaymeries, a blood brother of Jean-Paul in Mauriac's first novel, "although where we had there only a pencil sketch, here we have a Rembrandt engraving deeply etched with a magnificent distribution of lights and shadows." [6] The opening description of Fabien's childhood, watched over by the austere surveillance of his Jansenist mother, parallels and supplements the atmosphere of Mauriac's youth which we found in *La Robe prétexte* and in his autobiography *Commencements d'une vie.* "It was the habit of Madame Dézaymeries to rise at daybreak and, after Mass, to waken Fabien with a kiss. The kiss tasted of church and smelt of fog. . . . Each afternoon, when he got back from the park, she took him to the Cathedral for the Holy Hour." When his mother put him to bed after the evening prayer she "made the sign of the cross on his forehead with her thumb, crossed his hands on his breast, and listened while he repeated the ritual sentences that should guard him against the threat of sudden death." Young Fabien's life, like that of the youthful Mauriac, was bound up with the events of the church year. "When the candles were lit around the Manger he became a shepherd. . . . The bells on Resurrection Morning danced with the gaiety of life reborn. The air of the Month of Mary filled his nostrils with the scent of white roses. No somber weight lay upon his life. Austerity wreathed it like a mist shot through with sunlight." Like young Mauriac, Fabien tortured himself so much with religious scruples that sometimes he feared to have omitted some of his faults in confession. "Quite often he would deliberately munch a blade of grass before Mass, or swallow a mouthful of water when he cleaned his teeth, so as to avoid having to take communion, so fearful was he of committing sacrilege."

Yet into this pious household there came visits from a creature of quite another world, Fanny Barrett, an Irish woman who in her youth had been a friend of Fabien's mother. It would be difficult to imagine a greater contrast than that between these two, for Fanny was utterly contemptuous of religion, a gay divorcée with a checkered past thinking only of the carefree enjoyment of the present. Fabien falls under her spell at the age of eighteen, and his mother, full of misgivings, feels obliged to show her childhood friend the door. Unable to restore her son to his earlier serenity and faith, Mme Dézaymeries is now persuaded by her priest to send Fabien to Umbria and Rome. Instead, he goes to Venice where by chance he meets Fanny Barrett, about to commit suicide when abandoned by her second husband, Donald Larsen. In order to save her life Fabien allows Fanny to become his mistress and departs with her for Paris with alternating passion and loathing for his life of sin.

When Donald Larsen returns with his illegitimate daughter, a lovely, innocent girl named Colombe, Fabien promptly falls in love with her and breaks off in disgust his liaison with the aging courtesan Fanny. The latter, just as she had threatened, attempts to commit suicide but is revived. When Colombe is rushed off to a convent in Belgium, Fabien realizes with shame that he is still bound by ties of lust to Fanny, who, however, in her convalescence has been cured of her mad passion for the young lad. After an almost fatal attack of illness, Fabien is rescued by his sorrowing mother and taken back to the safe haven of his quiet province. As the author admits, however, "the real story of Fabien should, properly speaking, begin at this point, for all that had gone before was in the nature of a prologue." The reader is indeed entitled to wonder whether Fabien's repentance and reformation will be permanent and whether he will ever be able to regain his ardent faith.

It is not difficult to understand Mauriac's dislike for this early production. Tawdry and tasteless in its central episode—the liaison of a shopworn demimondaine with a student of twenty-two, melodramatic and preposterous in plot, Le Mal presents characters who are for the most part baffling and unconvincing. When we are transported to Venice and Paris, we find ourselves in the corrupt and vitiating ambiance of the courtesan and her cronies from the feverish world of the stage and dance.

Yet as is so often the case with Mauriac, like Antaeus of old, he seems to draw new strength whenever he touches the good earth—the land of balsam and pine where his boyhood vacations were spent. To the casual eye nothing could be more arid, uniform, and unprepossessing than this countryside. "Yet for all that it is a land of hidden springs with waters stained red by the stony soil. Ice-cold, they bubble up beneath the overshadowing alders and in the thickness of wild mint. Just so is the human heart, trained by the will to woo adversity, but thrilling to the call of love and wooed by grace." Never extraneous or superfluous, Mauriac's nature descriptions give us immediately the atmosphere which explains these austere ancestors from which Fabien sprang.

As straightly as by the high walls of the Catholic faith, by its un-breached and solid doctrine, the Dézaymeries lived hemmed about by the endless army of the pines which stood in serried ranks for forty miles. Only in that far distance did an ultimate ridge of sand lie as a barrier against the ocean surge. No austere heart is less responsive to the lure of passion than is this countryside to the magic of spring. The stunted oaks greet the winds of April with a rustle of dead leaves, and only the song of birds is eloquent of love.

When Mme Dézaymeries, anxious to do penance for having allowed Fanny to disturb the pious innocence of her son, went back in July to the Landes, it was "to a country buried in sand as in penitential ashes, with the stripped pines standing up like so many living examples of martyrdom humbly endured."

In summary we may say then of these five apprentice novels, so dissimilar in tone, that each is of interest primarily for its revelation concerning the author's formative years. Little by little he has been learning inventiveness of plot, creation of character other than autobiographical, observation of foibles and vices in society, and above all, poetic evocation of atmosphere. Yet so far we have not seen him construct a truly unified narrative nor create a single character who stands out in our memory. If Mauriac had died at thirty-seven before publishing his first masterpiece, *Le Baiser au lépreux*, it is unlikely that he would have left a mark on the history of French fiction.

CHAPTER 3

His Life: 1922 to the Present

I *The Religious Crisis*

ALTHOUGH Mauriac had long known and admired his fellow Bordelais, Jacques Rivière, it was not until 1922, the year of his fame with *Le Baiser au lépreux* and the publication by *La Nouvelle Revue Française* of his *Le Fleuve de feu* that he began his collaboration, for a time as dramatic editor, with this literary group. Matured and disillusioned by the suffering he had witnessed during World War I and by the humiliation he had personally experienced from his own physical weakness and uselessness as a participant, he published in 1923 the bitter *Genitrix* with its seething attack on obsessive mother love. These books, and in particular the passionate and burning *Fleuve de feu* called forth protests from the Catholic right—Mauriac even cites a remark of General Castelnau to the effect that he would not want to see the books of this man in the hands of his children.[1] L'abbé Bethléem in his *Revue des lectures* warned Catholic readers against this dangerous novelist, whose reputation as a morbid, if not pornographic, writer was to dog him in Catholic circles for many years. As Professor Jenkins has pointed out, Mauriac then decided to cease writing formally as a Catholic novelist and aimed instead at giving "an indirect apology for Christianity" through an objective rendering of the world which would show the danger from the absence of Christian devotion.[2]

From a literary point of view this change of emphasis was clearly successful, for *Le Désert de l'amour* in 1925 won the French Academy's Grand Prix du Roman, and *Thérèse Desqueyroux* (1927) was later adjudged by a literary jury in France as one of the best dozen novels written since 1900. With *Destins* in 1938, however, Mauriac reached a climacteric in his career, the "moment of choice" as he put it to Professor Jenkins, in regard to his reconciliation with the Church.

There were doubtless several reasons for the agonizing turmoil taking place in Mauriac's soul at this period. In addition to the condemnation of his work by many of his Catholic colleagues, he was involved in an extramarital experience which threatened for a time to destroy his marriage.[3] Earlier this same year he had published his *Life of Racine*, in which he so clearly identified his own struggle between worldliness and faith with that of Racine which culminated in his renunciation of the theater for a reconciliation with Port Royal and its austere precepts.

In the autumn of 1928 appeared Mauriac's *Souffrances du chrétien* in which we find the poignant lament: "Christianity makes no provision for the flesh, it suppresses it. 'God wants all,' Bossuet writes, and Pascal: 'Lord, I give thee all.' " [4] Then Mauriac attests the anguish experienced even by priests and persons consecrated to God, "that terror which they surmount but which often seizes them, of having renounced in vain the 'delightful and criminal usage of the world' of which Pascal speaks." We are struck by the contrast between the restless anxiety and despair found in *Souffrances*—Mauriac himself called it "the cry of a half-asphyxiated soul" [5]—and the radiant serenity apparent a few months later in its sequel, *Bonheur du chrétien*. Shall we agree with Mauriac's friend, the critic Charles du Bos, who claims that six weeks after the publication of *Souffrances* the conversion of Mauriac had taken place,[6] or shall we rather hold with Fidus who finds no evidence for such a dramatic change, but rather a new profundity in Mauriac after *Destins* which can be accounted for by "the maturity of approaching autumn, the reflections of a man who observes that his hair is growing white and that day is drawing to a close." [7]

Recently Mauriac has published his *Nouveaux Mémoires intérieurs* in which he has made the whole matter clear. It was Charles du Bos, a recent convert, who brought the anguished Mauriac in contact with the priest who converted him, Father X, himself a converted Jew. Mauriac's acknowledgment of debt to this priest is most eloquent.

At this moment of my life when I was in the ditch beside the road, bleeding, he had taken me on his shoulders, carried me to the Inn.

It had not been enough for him to confide me to the Innkeeper, he had remained with me, not leaving me for a moment, he had taken me to Solesme [monastery], then he rejoined me at Malagar and made with me the pilgrimage to Lourdes.[8]

It was at this same period that André Gide wrote Mauriac his famous letter, half-eulogistic, half-taunting, which was the impetus leading Mauriac to defend himself in *Dieu et Mammon*.

You rejoice that God, before taking possession of Racine, had left him time to write his plays, to write them *in spite of* the conversion. Therefore what you seek is the permission to write *Destins*; permission to be a Christian without having to burn your books—and that is what makes you write them in such a way that, although a Christian, you do not have to disavow them. All that (this reassuring compromise which allows one to love God without losing sight of Mammon) all that brings us this anguished conscience which lends so much attraction to your face, so much savor to your writings, and which must please so much those who, while abhorring sin, would be very sorry no longer to have to occupy themselves with sin. You know moreover that this would mean the end of literature, of yours in particular, and you are not enough of a Christian to be no longer a writer. Your great art consists of making accomplices of your readers. Your novels are less calculated to bring sinners back to Christianity than to remind Christians that there are on the earth other things than heaven.

I wrote one day, to the great indignation of some: "It is with beautiful sentiments that one makes bad literature." Yours is excellent, dear M. Mauriac. If I were more of a Christian I could doubtless follow you less.

Believe me, very amicably, your André Gide.

In *Dieu et Mammon* Mauriac undertakes to analyze his own conscience in reply to Gide's accusation. He disagrees with the view held by Maritain that a novelist must portray his characters objectively, without connivance, for in Mauriac's view a novelist is not a mere observer but a creator of fictitious life and must to some extent fuse and absorb himself in his creation. Mauriac is frank to admit that just as an honorable man may have unworthy sons, so the most honest novelist may be surprised to find the worst in him incarnated in his spiritual sons. He disagrees with Gide's statement that one cannot make good literature with beautiful sentiments, but agrees that these cannot be isolated, for only God can make saints, who are beyond the grasp of a novelist. While Racine was able to renounce writing, Mauriac is unable to resist "beings who move about in us, who take form, who demand the right to live. The need for writing finally becomes, in the man of letters, a sort of almost monstrous function which he can no longer escape." [9]

Yet Mauriac unconsciously showed the extent to which Gide's criticism struck home when he announced his decision to counter the attacks of his critics by improving the moral effect of his novels "by purifying the source."

II *Death's Shadow*

The first effect of this new religious orientation can be noticed in Mauriac's next novel. *Ce qui était perdu* (1929), called by Du Bos "a book of transition," is in Simon's opinion the first work in which the contradictory appeals of Mauriacian psychology are balanced: "on the one hand, the cruel analysis of souls abandoned to their sensations, their pride, their avarice; and on the other hand, the frankly admitted theme of a purification and an exaltation in supernatural charity." [10] Then in 1932 appeared one of Mauriac's greatest novels, *Le Noeud de vipères*, which Du Bos called "the accomplished success of a great Catholic novel."

Yet this year of his greatest triumph was also the year in which catastrophe suddenly cast its terrible shadow over Mauriac's life. One afternoon he consulted a throat specialist to help him dispel a certain hoarseness before a lecture engagement. "Like the blow of the fist which a rescuer gives a drowning man to prevent his thrashing about was the grim verdict. 'I have eighty chances out of a hundred to pull you out of this, but this is the last possible moment.'" Mauriac had cancer of the throat. Six months later the doctor felt certain of eventual success.

It was in a dark moment a few months later, when Mauriac believed he was having a fatal relapse, that his election to the French Academy occurred—which he modestly ascribed to his apparently mortal illness. Recalling an argument Henry Bordeaux had used some years later in favor of the election of the moribund Jacques Bainville—"we must not let him depart before becoming one of us"—Mauriac writes, "Thus with that obstinacy I have had all my life in taking advantage of everything, and even of sickness and death, this narrow passage ended for me in an election of marshal to the French Academy." [11]

One result of this close brush with death and his gradual convalescence during a long period of painful X-ray treatment was the necessity of communicating only by a hoarse whisper—a disability which is endured to this day. Another effect was his sudden discovery of a passion for music, and in particular for Mozart. Still another reaction was his decision to pay homage to his family, for their tender devotion during his long illness, by composing the autobiographical novel *Le Mystère Frontenac* (1933), for if he were to die at this time he did not wish to leave them with the stark blackness of *Le Noeud de vipères*. "I conceived *Le Mystère* as a hymn to the family. With *Le Mystère* I made honorable amends to my race." [12]

III *Journalism and the Campaign against Franco*

None of the novels Mauriac produced in the next seven years before World War II (*La Fin de la nuit*, 1935, *Les Anges noirs*, 1936, *Les Chemins de la mer*, 1939) are usually included among his masterpieces. Some critics have accounted for this diminished literary quality by stressing his changed religious attitude since his "conversion" and his effort to disarm the criticism of his Catholic colleagues. A more likely explanation would seem to be the increasing absorption of Mauriac, who was deeply stirred by the tragic events in Spain during this period, with his career as journalist.

We recall that during his last years in Bordeaux and his student days in Paris until 1907, Mauriac had embraced the progressive and unorthodox Catholic youth movement of Le Sillon, with its democratic interest in the worker class. Regarded by these workers with some coolness as "a man of letters" and as "a rich kid," Mauriac had left the movement with some disillusionment. Deeply influenced by the conservatism of his idol Barrès, a welcome guest in the aristocratic salons of the upper bourgeoisie, and inspired with a feeling of nationalism after World War I, Mauriac had had his earlier experience in journalism with the right-wing *Echo de Paris*. Now he returned to the liberal principles of his youth. "The Sillon had . . . given me, from the age of eighteen, that simple and clear outlook which, thirty years later, made me take sides against General Franco and against the Spanish hierarchy, first for the Basque people and clergy, then for the proletariat of Spain—and all that as a Catholic and because I was a Catholic."[13] After the massacre of Guernica, Mauriac together with Jacques Maritain and the ex-*Camelot du roi* Bernanos, bravely defended the cause of the Spanish republicans against Rome and the great majority of the French higher clergy. Mauriac became president of the Friends of the Basques and collaborated with the leftist Catholic weeklies, *Sept* and *Temps Présent* in an effort to "disengage the Church from a mortal compromise."[14]

IV *Mauriac and the Theater*

In an article in *Conférencia,* Mauriac confessed that he, like most other novelists, had been tempted by the stage but had feared the technical difficulties which this new world for him would involve. Nevertheless, when his friend Edouard Bourdet became administrator of the Théâtre Français and urged Mauriac to write for the theater, he welcomed this opportunity for enlarging his scope and entering upon a fresh career. The success of *Asmodée* in the winter of 1937–38 (100 performances) was generously ascribed by Mauriac to the helpful advice of Bourdet and the work of Jacques Copeau as stage manager.[15]

On March 12, 1938, a special performance of *Asmodée* in the Grand Théâtre, Bordeaux, given by the troupe of the Comédie Française, brought about a final reconciliation between Mauriac and his native city, which he had criticized so harshly in his novels. The mayor of Bordeaux had had special scenery painted for this gala performance, and a triumphant banquet took place, attended by all the notables of the city. When Mauriac was asked at the banquet whether there had been a theater in his Collège de Grand Lebrun, he answered in the affirmative and even admitted that he had once played the role of Elise in Racine's *Esther.*

V *Mauriac and World War II*

Mauriac's impassioned defense of the Spanish loyalists had as corollary his increasing distrust of Hitler and Mussolini who, he early realized, were using Spain as a proving ground for their bellicose plans to engulf Europe in a second world war. In his latest volume, *Mémoires politiques* (1967), many of these early warnings are reprinted under the heading "The Shadow of Hitler Spreads Over Us."

At the time the armistice of June, 1940 was concluded, Mauriac had already become, according to his friend Jean Blanzat, enemy number one for the German occupying forces and for the French collaborationists. "Ten echoes every week signaled his presence in the café, the theater, the street; lectures were given to designate him as a public poisoner. On every side he was ordered to keep silent, to disappear, to no longer exist." [16] Blanzat did not understand why Mauriac was not immediately thrown into a concentration camp. Jean Duché tells us that after meetings of the French Academy, Blanzat, Guéhenno, Paulhan and Mauriac used to meet at the Rohan café near the Théâtre Français. One day from a conversation between Paulhan, Decour, and Vildrac, *Les Lettres Françaises* was born. Mauriac and Guéhenno were not present but had already given their assurance of cooperation, and Mauriac became *Président d'honneur* of this courageous undertaking. The first number, ready in December, 1941, was seized; the following February Decour was arrested and shot.[17]

As early as 1941, Mauriac was writing his militant protest, *Le Cahier noir*, which appeared in the *Presses de Minuit* August 15, 1943, under the pseudonym of Forez. With passionate eloquence Mauriac attacked not only the cruelty of the invader but also the despicable sycophancy of the collaborationist magazines *L'Action Française*, *Gringoire* and *Je Suis Partout*. Refusing to despair of the ultimate victory of the human spirit over the tyranny of the oppressor, Mauriac wrote:

But we have made our choice; we wager against Machiavelli. We are among those who believe that man escapes from the law of devouring one another, and not only that he escapes from it but that all his dignity consists in the resistance he opposes to it with all his heart and with all his mind.[18]

An English translation appeared in London in May, 1944.

During these years of occupation Mauriac was also writing one of his great novels, *La Pharisienne* (1941), and a biography, *Sainte Marie de Cortone* (1945). We may gain a vivid idea of his life during this stormy period from his preface to the latter book.

The whole earth was covered with darkness. Was it in '41, in '42, in '43? Time no longer seemed divided; all of those winters formed nothing more than a black and frozen block in our minds. We lived them at Malagar in the womb of a monotonous terror. There was a German in every room. An enemy accordion groaned near the kitchen. Whether it was sunny or whether the wind streamed against the panes, the landscape was hopeless.

All the same it was necessary to write. One could not live on air only, nor on the outrages of a press that was drunk with rage. A Jesuit Father from Lyon claimed that it was I who was responsible for losing the war and that the reading of my novels had deterred French youth from fighting.

The martyrdom of the woman from Cortona distracted me from the martyrdom of my country: it made me unfaithful to that blood-soaked earth.

Then Mauriac added that many chapters had been interrupted because it was the hour of the London radio program, "Frenchman Speaking to Frenchmen," or because heavy boots were shaking the ceiling, or because "the fanfares of the great German Master were announcing on the radio a victory for the Reich." [19]

After *Le Cahier noir* appeared in 1943 it was unsafe for Mauriac to remain at Malagar, for his pseudonym of Forez was transparent. The attitude of the occupation authorities toward him is clearly indicated by a scurrilous article in *Je Suis Partout* (strikingly similar in tone to their condemnation of Saint-Exupéry) which concludes with these acerbic lines: "After, having coquetted for a time with the followers of Barrès and Maureás, this academician, this great landed proprietor began to pontificate among the bolshevik Christians to celebrate Red Spain, the Jewish war, De Gaulle, Roosevelt." [20] One evening in September, 1943, Mauriac returned to Paris and took refuge in the home of his friend Blanzat where he stayed several months. At one time in July, 1944 he hid from the Gestapo in open countryside in the region of Vémars, Seine et Oise. On August 25, 1944, during the liberation of Paris, while Mauriac was still in hiding, there appeared under his signature an article in *Le Figaro* expressing his homage to De Gaulle, under the title "Le Premier des Nôtres" (The First Among Us).

During the frenzied period of pursuit and execution of collaborationists after the Liberation, the voice of Mauriac was often raised in favor of mercy and forgiveness, until he received from his adversaries the sarcastic appelation "Saint François des As-

sises" (a sardonic pun of course on St. Francis of Assisi). His
efforts were not always successful, notably in the case of the well-
known critic Brasillach (who during the war had written a bitter
attack on Mauriac's work), but he was able to save Henri Béraud.

VI   The Nobel Prize

After 1946 Mauriac felt for a time that he had taken part long
enough in journalistic and political quarrels. "A last desire possessed me: to prove that the novelist in me was still alive. It was
an Indian summer and the old tree blossomed again in the midst
of winter." [21] In the decade after 1945 he produced three plays:
Les mal aimés (1945), Passage du Malin (1948), and Le Feu sur
la terre (1951); numerous essays and three novels, Le Sagouin
(1951), Galigaï (1952), and L'Agneau (1954). As he himself
wrote, his selection as laureate for the Nobel Prize in literature
was partly responsible for this literary renaissance.

As a presage of this great honor, on May 20, 1952, Mauriac was
received in the Grand Théâtre as a member of the Academy of
Sciences, Belles Lettres and Arts of Bordeaux, whose President
was his elder brother Pierre Mauriac, Dean of the Faculty of
Medicine. He was following in the footsteps of another wine
grower on the banks of the Garonne, also a member of both Acad-
emies, his compatriot Montesquieu. In this ultimate reconciliation
with his city, Mauriac said in his response: "I recall having written one day: 'I love Bordeaux like myself; I hate it like myself.' It
is indeed this interpenetration, if I dare say so, of the poet and the
city where he was born, which explains his impulses of love, but
also his irritations, his rancors." And Mauriac then confessed that
Paris had done nothing for him but bring forth the riches accumu-
lated during the twenty years he had lived in Bordeaux and under
the pines of Saint-Symphorien and the arbors of Malagar.

In addition to Mauriac, the Nobel committee was considering
two other names, the Spaniard Ramon Menendez Pidal and the
Englishman Graham Greene, whom many considered a disciple of
Mauriac. In an interview with Paul Guth after his election, Mauriac modestly suggested that his selection was something of an
injustice to Duhamel, Jules Romains, André Maurois and especially to Claudel who towers above them all. (Incidentally the
jealousy aroused in Claudel by this choice seems to have amused
Mauriac, who repeated to me with a chuckle Claudel's indignant

reaction: "What, they give this international prize to this regionalist!")

Mauriac's acceptance speech in Stockholm, December 10, 1952, may be compared in importance to that memorable one delivered on a similar occasion some four years later by Albert Camus. Beginning modestly with an expression of surprise that the little world of his boyhood should have interested foreign readers, Mauriac nevertheless admits that the same phenomenon was true for George Eliot, Charles Dickens, Leo Tolstoi, and Selma Lagerlöf. "The gift of the novelist goes back precisely to the power of making evident the universality of this narrow world in which we have learned to love and to suffer." (How many other names Mauriac might have mentioned to prove his contention, among them Thomas Hardy, William Faulkner, and Jean Giono.)

Then Mauriac expresses his surprise that so many of his readers have found his works somber. "Yet the works which have remained alive in the memory of men are those which have covered the entire human drama and which have not tried to escape from the evidence of irremediable solitude in the midst of which each one of us has had to confront his destiny up to death, that last solitude, since finally we shall die alone." Every time a woman tries to poison her husband or strangle a lover, Mauriac is told, "there is a subject for you. I pass for keeping a sort of museum of horrors. I am a specialist in monsters."

Yet in his Christian faith Mauriac has been possessed of a great hope which pierces the shadows he has described. He feels that his characters differ from others in fiction because they have a soul. "Any writer who has maintained in the center of his work the human creature made in the image of the Father, redeemed by the Son, illumined by the Spirit, I cannot see in him a master of despair, however somber his painting may be." And if Mauriac is obsessed by evil, he is also obsessed by purity, by childhood. He regrets that critics have not observed the important role that children play in his works. "They see the vipers of my novels, they do not see the doves which nestle there also in more than one chapter, because with me childhood is the lost paradise and leads to the mystery of evil."

VII   *Mauriac, Algeria, and De Gaulle*

After receiving the Nobel Prize, Mauriac conceived the idea, since *La Nouvelle Revue Française* had disappeared, of founding a new review, *La Table Ronde,* which would be open to the best writers of both Right and Left. Albert Camus did collaborate on the first number, but Mauriac, assisted by Thierry Maulnier, was soon left with only the writers of the Right and of the extreme Right, far removed from Mauriac's own political principles. Furthermore the N.R.F., with the title *Nouvelle Nouvelle Revue Française,* then reappeared.

It was on his descent from the train from Stockholm that Mauriac learned of the trouble in North Africa, which began with the events in Morocco. Mauriac allied himself with young Catholics on the Left to found the movement France-Maghreb, which became one of the foundations on which General De Gaulle was able to build his policy.[22] Since Mauriac's weekly *Bloc-Notes* with their denunciations of French colonialism were now an embarrassment to *Le Figaro,* Mauriac transferred his articles to the new liberal publication of J. J. Servan-Schreiber. When De Gaulle returned to power in 1958 and set French policy on a new course in regard to independence for Algeria, Mauriac rallied to his support. In November of that year Mauriac was elevated to the rank of Grand Croix de la Légion d'Honneur on the personal recommendation of General De Gaulle.

In the early 1960's, the antagonism of the Organisation de l'Armée Secrète against De Gaulle's anti-colonial policy was at its height, and the *"plastiqueurs"* were taking vengeance on all who supported De Gaulle (and even in at least one case, attempting to assassinate De Gaulle himself). An effort was made to blow up the country home of Mauriac at Malagar, which was foiled fortunately by the appearance on the scene of the huge watchdog in time to rout the invaders. When I interviewed Mauriac in the summer of 1962, I noticed a French policeman marching to and fro in front of his apartment; he confirmed to me that the government, feeling him to be in danger, had stationed a security officer permanently there.

The latest years of Mauriac's life have been comparatively uneventful, marked by continuous literary activity with his weekly *Bloc-Notes* for *Le Figaro Littéraire* (and for a time his weekly

article concerning television). His eightieth birthday was celebrated by a complete issue of *Le Figaro Littéraire* with eulogies
from various critics. Almost every year has seen the appearance of
a new volume from his pen, among them a eulogistic biography of
De Gaulle (1964) and various personal memoirs: *Memoires
intérieurs* (1959), *Ce que je crois* (1962), *Nouveaux Mémoires
intérieurs* (1965), and *Mémoires politiques* (1967).

CHAPTER 4

The Minor Novels

I   Le Fleuve de feu (*1923*)

WE WOULD not gain a complete idea of Mauriac as a novelist by limiting our discussion to his half-dozen masterpieces which alone seem destined for immortality. None of his less successful novels is entirely lacking in interest and some of them contain passages of nature description, psychological penetration, and tenseness of narration almost equal to the best that he has produced. Few of these elements, however, can be observed in *Le Fleuve de feu* (The River of Fire), one of the weakest of his books, which marks an almost unbelievable decline between two of his most perfect works, *Le Baiser au lépreux* and *Genitrix*.

The rather banal plot can be summarized briefly. Daniel Trasis, a blasé young businessman, is spending a rather boring vacation in a small hotel in the Pyrenees when his attention is aroused by the arrival of an attractive girl of twenty-six, Gisèle de Plailly, who seems to him the type of ingenuous purity worthy of his conquest. She on her part is awaiting the coming of an older friend, Mme de Villeron, with Marie, a six-year-old girl, whose sudden illness has delayed their trip. During the next few days we observe the increasing interest of Gisèle for Daniel, whom she alternately attracts and repels. When Mme de Villeron finally makes her appearance with Marie, the somewhat raucous laughter of the little girl, so similar in quality to that of Gisèle, makes Daniel suspect that Marie may be Gisèle's illegitimate daughter. Mme de Villeron in her capacity as watchdog over Gisèle soon becomes aware of the latter's infatuation with Daniel and sets their departure for an early hour the next morning.

In his bedroom that night, Daniel becomes aware that a letter is being pushed under his door; he rushes out in time to catch Gisèle and pull her into the room. Now ensues the most passionate episode of the novel as Gisèle confesses her love and willingly spends the night with Daniel. Mme de Villeron discovers Gisèle's bed undisturbed and observes the light under Daniel's door. She listens with anguish to the amorous reactions of the lovers, and when Gisèle emerges at early dawn, throws a mantle over her shoulders and prepares for their departure.

As the trio ride on the train to Paris, the author gives us a flashback which enlightens us about Gisèle's past. During World War I Gisèle was accustomed to escape almost daily from her niggardly and domineering father by taking a local train to Paris, ostensibly to obtain cheaper provisions. On one such occasion she was seduced by a young soldier, who returned to the trenches to his death after his five-day leave. When the baby Marie was born, Mme de Villeron, to spare Gisèle the shame of illegitimacy, had adopted Marie as a war orphan, thereby acquiring a hold over her protégée Gisèle.

In the final scene of the novel we see Gisèle, won back to the faith and repentant as she thinks Daniel has abandoned her, transformed into a sort of angel of mercy caring for the children of the village who attend mass in the neglected and almost ruined church. Daniel, returning at last to carry her off, is so impressed by the sanctity of the church service and the conversion of Gisèle that he retreats unseen to the door of the church, and he "bathed his hand in the holy water, touched his forehead, his breast, his shoulders, went away."

There is little in this novel to recall the charm of Mauriac's earlier *Le Baiser au lépreux*, except perhaps for occasional descriptive passages related to the picturesque setting in the Pyrenees: the dark shadows of the distant mountains, the tinkling of cowbells, the mist floating over the valleys, the murmur of rushing waters, and the sound of a solitary cricket in the grass. In delineating the psychology of the principal characters, Mauriac's sureness of touch seems to have deserted him. Daniel, the sole male protagonist, is an unconvincing medley of brutal sensuality with an obsession for purity. He wavers between the two great influences of his life: his memory of the virtuous Marie Ransinange who had fulfilled her oath to enter a convent if Daniel's life should be spared in the war, and his endeavor to imitate the coarse immorality of his friend Raymond Courrèges (whom we shall meet in *Le Désert de l'amour*). Mme de Villeron, in some respects a saintly

creature in her disdain for the joys of the flesh and her zealous
devotion to Gisèle and Marie, is perhaps unconsciously dominated
by her pride in having plucked this brand from the burning.
Gisèle de Plailly, the rather tawdry and tarnished heroine, does
not quite ring true in her sudden descent into "the river of fire" to
give herself passionately to a man she scarcely knew, then her
ascension so soon afterward to an aura of saintliness and religious
devotion.

Except for the one central episode of passion which illustrates
with startling vividness the title of the work, the plot is rather
awkwardly developed. The flashback in the train, which outlines
in great detail the early temptation and fall of the heroine, is so
long that we lose interest in the outcome of Gisèle's later adventure. Almost all critics have decried the artificiality of the denouement, a *coup de théâtre* insufficiently prepared by what we have
previously learned of the character. The novel is preceded by a
quotation from Saint John: "Everything in the world is concupis-
cence of the flesh, or of the eyes, or pride of life," followed by
similar quotations from Pascal and Bossuet. It must be said that
this demonstration of the gross sensuality of the protagonists contrasts strangely with the artificial, almost saccharine conclusion.

II   Destins (1928)

There are few of Mauriac's novels which have not been preferred by at least one critic, and *Destins* (The Lines of Life) is no
exception, for André Bellesort considered it the greatest and most
perfect of his works.[1] It is indeed a powerful novel, far superior to
Le Fleuve de feu in character portrayal and poetic atmosphere,
but in my opinion it just misses greatness.

As so often in Mauriac's novels, we find here a decided antithe-
sis between two worlds: the postwar frenzy, dissipation, and
moral laxity of Parisian society, and the unchanging conservatism
of the landholders in the region of the Garonne. Bob Lagave,
handsome but dissolute son of the austere and materialistic func-
tionary Augustin Lagave, has been forced by a severe attack of
pleurisy to abandon his adventures in high society in order to
recuperate at home. Angered by the unending stream of callers
representing all facets of society from a princess down to shady
characters from the underworld, Augustin decides to send his son
to regain his health at the home of old grandmother Lagave, a

peasant woman of stern morality formerly in the service of the
Gornac family, whose vast estates of vineyards and forest lie
nearby. Somewhat to his father's surprise, Bob accedes willingly
to this proposal, for he knows that the girl with whom he is in
love, Paule de la Sesque, is spending the summer at Arcachon,
only eighty kilometers away.

Bob passes most of his time convalescing on the porch of the
Gornac home, watched over with loving care by Elisabeth the
forty-eight-year-old widow of old Gornac's son. With his seduc-
tive charm, which few women have been able to resist, Bob persuades Elisabeth to accept the possibility of an automobile breakdown which will present the opportunity for his sweetheart Paule
to spend the night at the Gornac mansion. The carefully planned
"breakdown" occurs, Paule is presented to Elisabeth as his fiancée,
the two lovers leave to have dinner in the hotel at Langon, and
Elisabeth succeeds in getting old Gornac to retire so that he will
not hear their return. Unfortunately, however, her son Pierre, a
fanatic religionist, comes home just in time to catch sight of the
lovers in the garden, is scandalized to find his mother in sympathy
with such an arrangement, and proceeds to tell Paule all he knows
or has heard concerning the unsavory and licentious past of her
would-be fiancé. Paule, half-convinced and heart-stricken, plans
to leave early next morning, without seeing Bob again, in order to
verify the scurrilous rumors. All that Elisabeth can obtain from
her is her promise to return in a fortnight.

The next morning Bob is aghast to find that Paule has left,
forces Pierre to confess that he has warned her against marriage
with him, knocks the young seminarian unconscious, and returns
to grandmother Lagave's to await with despair and foreboding
the promised return of Paule, who represents to him his one hope
of settling down to a happy and normal life. He writes her a letter
which receives no answer. Stupefying himself with brandy, he receives Elisabeth with a frantic embrace; when she indignantly re-
pulses him, he tells her she will regret it some day. On the eight-
eenth day without the return of Paule, a luxurious auto drives up,
filled with friends of his dissipated years in Paris. They persuade
Bob to leave with them on a three-day trip to Deauville. On the
following day Paule does indeed arrive, convinced that the worst
revelations about Bob's past are all too true, but unable to discard
her love for him even though marriage is now out of the question.

Next day comes a telegram from Augustin Lagave in Paris, stating that Bob has been killed in an auto accident and that he and his wife are bringing the body to Langon for burial in the family vault. To the great relief of Pierre, who has been wondering if he had done the right thing in warning Paule, he receives word that Bob lived for two hours after the accident and in the last fifteen minutes of his life manifested to a priest his complete conversion and repentance. Poor Elisabeth, conscious now that she has experienced love for the first time in her life in her adoration of Bob, finds herself indifferent to the departure of her son Pierre as he leaves for missionary work in Africa. With a heavy heart, she seeks to adjust herself to the monotony of daily life on the estate she must manage and which has lost all meaning for her.

In *Destins* we see Mauriac's gift for irony at its best. Earlier in the story while old Gornac and his daughter-in-law were en route back to Viridis at the news of the grave accident to Prudent, Elisabeth's husband, Gornac could not refrain from asking her if she had remembered to order the casks for the vintage. At the same time Elisabeth, despite her real sorrow at the prospect of approaching widowhood, could not keep her thoughts from wandering to the consideration of her legal rights to the inheritance. When Augustin wrote concerning plans for his son's burial he included this reflection so typical in its gross materialism: "In spite of the exorbitant price for this sort of transport, I have decided that the body of my son shall be laid to rest at Viridis." And finally, when Augustin, fearing that no one would be present for the funeral ceremony in Paris of his "worthless" son, invited specially all his employees and superiors at the ministry, he was filled with amazement at the stream of aristocratic faces and the profusion of roses and funeral wreaths which inundated the church. "How much he was loved," thought Mme Lagave in tears.

The setting in which most of the story is laid reminds us of the early novel *La Chair et le sang*, since it too takes place amid the vineyards of Viridis above the Garonne, near Mauriac's own home of Malagar above Langon. This familiar setting bathes the novel in typically Mauriacian warmth and color. Though lyrical descriptions of natural beauty are subdued in comparison with those of the earlier work, on the occasion of Bob's despair when abandoned by Paule Mauriac orchestrates the theme of hopelessness by introducing a parallel note from nature. "But Bob appeared stunned and fixed his eyes obstinately on the dull horizon, a sky the color of slate. The west wind brought the noise of church bells, the rumbling of trains which foretells the rain at Viridis. He looked at this immense countryside, mute and empty." In his lonely waiting for Paule's return, "he measured with desolate glance this plain, livid and dormant under a dark sky, a sky like the end of the world, rent at brief intervals by flashes of lightning on the horizon." Unlike many denouements in which Mauriac seems to hurry his development, the funeral scene in the church of Langon is full of poignant beauty and majesty, imbued with a grave harmony which reminds one critic of Chopin and Schumann:

What a page is that prayer, those sobs of Elisabeth in the country church where only a mother watches over the coffin of her son. Funeral march in the highest, most classic style; and it is Chopin as well as Schumann that one must invoke now, since the pangs of grief are followed now, in life which goes on, by the appeasement of indifference and mediocrity which set in once more.[2]

The title of this work can be explained readily enough by Mauriac's conviction of the responsibility which lies on each one of us in regard to our influence, for good or for evil, over our fellow men.

We think that a being has disappeared from our life; we seal his memory with a stone bearing no epitaph; we give him up to oblivion; we go back home, our heart delivered, into our existence before his coming; everything is just as if he had not been. But it does not depend on us to efface any trace. The imprints of man upon man are eternal, and no destiny has ever crossed our own with impunity.

The implications of this philosophy in *Destins* are numerous. The tragedy would not have occurred if Elisabeth had not been won over by Bob's youthful charm to act as hostess for the amorous engagement. If she had not overslept the following morning, contrary to her lifelong habit, she could have warned Bob of Pierre's treachery and given him the possibility of persuading Paule to stay. If Pierre had not returned just at the wrong time and been so scandalized by the love affair, he would not have caused Paule's sudden departure. If Paule had answered Bob's pitiful letter or had even returned in a fortnight as she had promised, she would have found him patiently waiting. And finally, if Bob's shady cronies from Paris had not reached him in their auto just as he had abandoned all hope for Paule's return, he would not have embarked on the fatal ride which resulted in his flaming death. All of these interrelationships are skillfully—perhaps too skillfully—intermingled to illustrate this theme of responsibility.

Yet there is another aspect of the novel which suggests ambiguities and confusion of purpose in the mind of the author. At first reading, Pierre, the bookish, austere young seminarian whose spreading of rumors concerning Bob's licentious past precipitates the rupture between the young lovers, would seem to represent an attack upon religious fanaticism by the author. Our sympathy goes instinctively to Bob, so youthful and appealing in spite of his early immersion in corrupt and vitiated aristocratic society; to the graceful and sprightly Paule whose rustic origins have preserved her to some extent from the cynicism of her comrades; and especially to the poignant figure of Elisabeth, who resembles Eugénie Grandet in her mingling of practicality and administrative competence with a latent capacity for love and tenderness. *Destins* is primarily a study of *moeurs* rather than an analysis of character. Yet it is the subtle shading of Mauriac's delineation of the autumnal flowering of passion in the middle-aged Elisabeth—presaging his similar study of Marcelle's infatuation with young Harry Fanning in his play *Asmodée* a decade later—which remains longest in the reader's memory.

Is this contrast between the demands of the senses, so evident in Bob, Paule, and Elisabeth, and the harsh and domineering asceticism of the fanatical mystic Pierre, one more illustration of the dichotomy we have seen before in the author, torn between the conflicting pressures of sensual passion and craving for purity? We should remember that *Destins*, published in 1928 a few months before the anguished outpourings of his *Souffrances du chrétien*, belongs to perhaps the darkest period of his life. Tormented on the one hand by reproaches of immorality from his Catholic friends, he was caught, as has been mentioned, at the same time in the grip of an extra-marital passion which threatened to destroy his domestic tranquillity. If we examine the character of Pierre more closely we shall find that he is perhaps in the eyes of the author a tragic rather than a repellent figure, condemned to an inner solitude and dependence on sainthood because of his unattractive physical appearance, his impracticality, and his disdain for material things. He is not a hypocrite, for he realizes that jealousy of Bob's boyish charm and pride for having saved Paule from a disastrous marriage had been partly responsible for his decision to warn her about Bob's past. For many days he had asked himself remorsefully whether his action was justifiable, and it is only when he learns of Bob's last-minute repentance that he rejoices at having been God's chosen instrument for this conversion. His rejoicing, on the other hand, is contrasted with the hopeless melancholy and bitter resentment of his mother, who feels that all beauty and meaning have been erased from her life. Here we have the impression that Mauriac is adrift between two competing philosophies; it is this ambivalence and confusion of moral outlook which alone perhaps keep us from ranking *Destins* among his greatest novels.

III   Ce qui était perdu (*1930*)

Ce qui était perdu (That Which Was Lost) is the first novel of Mauriac after his "conversion." Although the work belongs to his third and final period which has been called that of "the Catholic novelist," it is still, like *Destins*, a novel of transition. According to his friend Charles Du Bos, it was to have been called *Pygmalion*, intended primarily as a study of incest.[3] This theme is still present in the final version in the relation of brother and sister, Alain and Tota, but reduced to the status merely of unfounded suspicion, which nevertheless in the insinuations of the evil friend Hervé plays a decisive role in the outcome. The unity of this work suffers somewhat in its alternation of interest between two families: on the one hand, Marcel, his wife Tota, and her brother Alain; on the other, Hervé, his desperately ill wife Irène, and her pious mother-in-law, Mme de Blenange. Geographically also, as in *Destins*, we find a similar alternation between the depraved society life of Paris and the rustic château near Bordeaux where Alain and Tota had grown up. But in this case one cannot speak of contrast between darkness and sunshine, for the rural setting is that of a ruined, forsaken château in which the half-mad, paralytic father casts a baleful gloom over all the family.

As the story begins, Alain and Tota are about to arrive in Paris on their voyage from l'Entre-deux-mers. While Marcel, Tota's husband of a few months, awaits their coming, he is visited by his false friend the *boulevardier* Hervé, whose evil genius prompts him always to see wickedness and vice in all who surround him. He implants in Marcel the horrible thought that the unusual interest between brother and sister may well represent conscious, or at least unconscious, incest.

Irène, the docile and loving invalid wife of Hervé, accidentally overhears a conversation between Hervé and Marcel in which her husband asks Marcel to corroborate a lie to explain his intended absence over the weekend to indulge his illicit pleasures. She confesses her involuntary eavesdropping to Hervé and implores him to make her the sacrifice of remaining at her bedside. Realizing from her solemn plea that his action may have a vital significance, Hervé reads aloud to his wife from her favorite philosopher Nietzsche, but when he observes that she has dozed off as a result of her tranquillizers, he slips quietly out of the house. Hearing the door click, Irène wakens and realizes her desertion and the broken promise of her profligate husband. She decides that this is the sign she has awaited and takes an overdose of gardenal tablets. When Hervé returns and finds her lifeless body, his first reaction is one of jubilation and freedom rather than of remorse. Later, going to his mother's house, he is touched by the old woman's piety and remorse for not having prevented the tragedy, and he buries his head in his mother's lap, sobbing as he used to do as a child.

In the meantime, Marcel has gone off with his former mistress, Marie Chavès, whom he had previously infected with his own craving for drugs. Tota, horrified by the possibility that Marcel's accusation of incest might have some foundation, has now decided to give herself to a dissolute young aristocrat of English descent. Fortunately, Alain arrives just in time to save her, takes her back with him to the ancestral château where the terrible father has died, and with a newfound radiance confides in her his plan to become a priest.

Thus the novel ends leaving the reader somewhat perplexed over the future of these characters. Will Hervé's repentance be enduring? Will Marcel, after having restored Marie Chavès to a normal existence, return to his wife Tota? Will the latter be able to adjust herself to a new life without her brother and forgive her husband for his horrible suspicion? In the case of Alain's future, at least, we shall have the answer in a later novel. In regard to Mau-

riac's tendency to take up again certain characters in later novels
it should be mentioned that the reader of *Ce qui était perdu*
catches a short glimpse of Mauriac's famous Thérèse Desqueyroux
sobbing in despair on a park bench after abandonment by a lover.
She is taken back to her hotel by Alain, a total stranger who was
touched by her misery—an incident which has no connection
whatever with the progress of this novel and shows only the preoccupation of the author with his favorite character.

We must, I think, agree with North in his inability to understand why Charles Du Bos considered this the first of Mauriac's so-
called Catholic novels, in which he observes for the first time the
absence of any "connivance" of the author with the guilty passions
of his characters. Perhaps North is correct when he suggests that
the only justification for the attitude of Du Bos is that "here, for
the first time the novelist, like an 18th century dramatist, makes
all the sins take place in the wings and does not represent them on
the stage." [4] We may agree also with Mauriac's usually benevo-
lent critic Jaloux that when old Mme Blenange confesses to the
priest her involuntary discouragement of Irène's acceptance of
the faith and her remorse for not having prevented the tragedy,
the priest's response does not carry conviction: "Rejoice my daughter. . . . I can only repeat to you in trembling what the Master
inspires me to tell you: 'She was absent, but I was there.'" Jaloux
thought it strange that Irène could find the road to salvation only
in suicide, and that a priest could assure us of her salvation. "I am
willing to believe that the designs of God are unfathomable, but
we are dealing here with the designs of M. Mauriac and not with
those of God." [5]

Ce qui était perdu offers certain individual scenes of dramatic
intensity and pathos. Yet because of its somber atmosphere of vice
and cruel inhumanity from which only the noble dignity of Irène,
the harsh piety of Mme Blenange, and the sudden transformation
of Alain offer a brief respite, because also of the fragmentary and
unconnected structure of the plot with its unconvincing denouement, this work must be ranked as one of the weakest of Mauriac's minor novels.

IV   Le Mystère Frontenac (*1933*)

Soon after his election in 1932 as president of the Society of
Men of Letters, Mauriac underwent, as we have seen, a serious

illness culminating in an operation which left his vocal chords seriously impaired. Grateful for their solicitude and affection, Mauriac wished to express his gratitude to his loved ones by composing this volume, which is less a novel than a collection of *"mémoires imaginaires"* covering the period of his adolescence in Bordeaux and on the family estate near Langon which he here calls Bourideys. "I conceived *Le Mystère* as a hymn to the family on the morrow of a grave operation and illness during which my family had surrounded me with such tender solicitude. If I had died, I should not have wished *Le Noeud* to be the last of my works." [6] Mauriac's first idea had been to call this work *Nid de Colombes* (Nest of Doves), which would have emphasized the sharp contrast in tone with the preceding novel. We may well prefer the later title, since the members of this family, for all their mutual affection, had little in common with *colombes*.

Part I, almost devoid of incident, is devoted to a portrayal of the family in Bordeaux and the lovely surroundings of their rustic paradise in the Landes. Michel Frontenac at his death had left his widow Blanche with the responsibility of raising five children: Jean-Louis the elder, José, little Yves, and the two daughters Danièle and Marie (who play almost no role in the story). Their uncle Xavier, an agnostic republican devoted to his brother's memory and the children's welfare, has a law office in Angoulême but comes every fortnight to oversee the accounts of the family's lumber company. Uncle Xavier has a secret which he guards anxiously from the family: he has a mistress, an ignorant woman of humble extraction whom he dare not introduce to the family for fear of all the scandal that would ensue. The only happenings in this part of the novel, embellished with some of Mauriac's most felicitous descriptions of nature and analysis of character, are: discovery of little Yves's poetic vocation by his sympathetic brother Jean-Louis, and the latter's renunciation of his studies for the doctorate in philosophy so that he could take his place in the business world as partner in the family firm. (Though this represented a real sacrifice on the part of the studious lad, it did offer as compensation the opportunity for marrying the girl he loved and founding a family.)

In Part II we follow Yves to Paris to continue his literary career. Enmeshed before long in a social whirl, he accompanies a group of young socialites and while passing through Bordeaux manages to spend fifteen minutes with his mother. On the return trip he yields only too readily to the impatience of his comrades and fails to make the effort for another visit to Blanche. Back in Paris he is soon caught up again in his frivolous social life, when suddenly he receives a visit from Jean-Louis who first announces that their mother is very ill, then admits sadly that he has come to take Yves back with him to her funeral. In spite of his very real sorrow and remorse for not visiting her again while passing through Bordeaux (a reminiscence of Mauriac's own experience), Yves can scarcely keep his mind off the girl with whom he is infatuated, whom he plans to meet again in Paris next autumn. Uncle Xavier falls desperately ill, and contrary to his instructions, his mistress Josépha summons all the Frontenac clan to his bedside—all, that is, except José, the black sheep of the family, who after squandering part of the inheritance upon a mistress had been persuaded to redeem himself by entering military service in Morocco. Yves discovers the unfaithfulness of the girl he loves, and, discouraged by his lack of literary success, takes an overdose of sleeping powder. Almost miraculously, however, Jean-Louis has had a presentiment that Yves needs his presence in Paris, leaves a business engagement involving perhaps a hundred-thousand-franc sale, and arrives at Yves's apartment in time to nurse him back to health. Thus the novel ends with this gleam of hope: "The Frontenac mystery was escaping destruction, for it was a ray of the eternal love reflected through a race."

In spite of the sincere emotion of the author which we experience in the second half of the novel, particularly in the tragic scenes of Blanche Frontenac's funeral and the pathos of Xavier's anguish as he realizes on his deathbed that his guilty secret has been disclosed to his family, there is an atmosphere of sentimentality and melodrama in the sufferings of Yves. The first half of the novel, with its graphic and moving picture of the Frontenac household, is far superior. Much of the quiet charm distilled from these pages comes from the delicate touches of nature description, in which storm and forest fire are almost uniquely absent.

The springtime was hovering in this winter twilight like a being one feels close at hand but does not see. The boy thought he could hold his breath and, all at once, there was nothing; it was cold. The four o'clock light, for a brief instant, caressed the trunks, the bark of the

pine trees glistened like scales, their gluey wounds captured the last
rays of the sun. Then, suddenly, all was extinguished; the west wind
drove along heavy clouds which skimmed the tops of the trees, and
it wrested from this somber throng a long lament.

If the two girls and the profligate José are only lightly sketched,
the majestic and lovely figure of the mother, Blanche Frontenac,
is admirably painted in her noble devotion to the welfare of her
little brood. Uncle Xavier, likewise, is an unforgettable character
in his disinterestedness which allows him to renounce his share of
the inheritance in favor of the children. Too weak to free himself
from a liaison which he realizes is shameful, he forces both his
mistress and himself to live on a pittance in order not to impair
the financial security of the children, and he seeks to hide his
ménage in order not to bring discredit upon the family. Even his
mistress Josépha achieves a certain nobility in her worship for this
family whose members she has learned to love vicariously. Jean-
Louis has replaced his father as the head of the family, strong and
straight as an oak, bringing to business his concern for the weak
and underprivileged. His sensitivity to poetic beauty is shown by
his encouragement of Yves's literary efforts, and he is willing to
throw to the winds all thought of financial gain when it is time to
save his beloved brother from self-destruction. Though Yves himself is very appealing in his poetic vocation and his shyness in
disclosing his literary work from fear of ridicule, several critics
have complained that Mauriac should have chosen a less self-
centered egotist to carry the burden of the action.

Mauriac affirmed to this writer that two of the characters in this
novel, Blanche Frontenac (his mother) and Uncle Xavier (his
uncle Louis Mauriac) were drawn directly from life, almost
without modification. Even if we had not suspected from an early
mention of Yves' drooping eyelid that he is a subjective portrait,
Mauriac's admission would be convincing. "For Yves, he is another myself, more somber, more despairing, as I would have been
had I not founded a happy family." [7] His brothers and his sister,
on the other hand, have been completely altered. As he wrote in
the article mentioned above:

Yes, Le Mystère constitutes a chapter of my memories. Everything
in it is true, but it is a novel and everything in it, if not invented, is

at least transposed. The themes borrowed from my real life benefit from an orchestration which has kept those who were the actors and witnesses from recognizing it. I recall my astonishment and sorrow when I received by the same mail, the day after the book's publication, several irritated letters from my close kin. Insensible to this poetry of our common past which I had decanted, so to speak, in order to reject the deposit and the dregs, they considered as a treason and a lie my infidelity to the letter of our destiny.

Though one Anglican critic strangely enough considers *Le Mystère Frontenac* the most totally successful of Mauriac's novels[8] it is too sentimental and melodramatic, too episodic and lacking in its technique of construction, I think, to rank among his truly great works. The most one can say in its defense is that it possesses a serenity, a charm, and above all a highly personal subjectivity which make it thoroughly readable.

V Les Anges noirs (1936)

Les Anges noirs (The Dark Angels) is the first novel of Mauriac to appear in serial form (in the magazine *Gringoire*), and perhaps this accounts in part for its complicated plot and almost hair-raising intensity. In his *Le Romancier et ses personnages* published about this time, Mauriac had written: "Sometimes I had wondered if it would be possible for me to write a detective novel, a serial, with the sole purpose of entertaining the reader and keeping him breathless. Perhaps I shall do this, but as a 'pensum.'" [9] Obviously the novel is much more than this, since it includes not only a realistic portrait of rural cupidity but also illustrates one of Mauriac's favorite themes: the ultimate conversion of a sinner through Divine Grace. Nevertheless, its aspect of *roman policier* or "Catholic thriller" has been noted by most critics.

Though the novel is not exempt from certain incongruities and contradictions in plot construction, Mauriac has attained here a certain classic unity of form by his division of the narrative into three parts: prologue, novel proper, and epilogue. In the long prologue consisting of a forty-two-page letter of confession from the villain-hero Gradère to the young village priest, Alain Forcas, the author gives us all the background we need for understanding the rapid unfolding of tragedy. Gradère, son of a sharecropper and steward of the Peloueyre family (another instance, like that of our renewed acquaintance with Alain, of Mauriac's tendency to bring

in, like Balzac, characters from an earlier novel to strengthen the
unity of his whole work) because of his quick intelligence, physical charm, and appeal for all around him has been awarded a
scholarship in the seminary. Yet even at this early age, Gradère
felt within himself a definite propensity for hypocrisy and evil. He
corrupted one of the aristocratic Du Buch girls, Adila, who went
to Bilboa to hide the illegitimate birth of their son, Andrès. During
her absence from the country, Gradère had become entangled in a
sordid liaison with a disreputable character, Aline, who hence-
forth will exercise a hold over him because of her knowledge of
his shady business practices. Desperate for money, Gradère returned from Paris to the little town of Liogeats in the Landes,
prepared to marry his former mistress Adila. Shocked by her loss
of physical charm he became suddenly infatuated with her
younger cousin Mathilde, but could not marry her because Adila
insisted that he fulfill his agreement to marry her and thereby
make Andrès legitimate. Mathilde then married an elderly farmer,
Symphorien Desbats, to whom she bore a daughter, Catherine.
After the death of Adila, Mathilde adopted the young Andrès, to
whom she became more attached than to her own daughter. Gradère, hoping to escape from the clutches of Aline, planned to visit
Desbats to prevent him from acquiring the two remaining estates
of Andrès until he should sign a contract for the marriage of his
daughter Catherine with Andrès. And now we are ready for the
rapidly developing events of the novel proper.

As Gradère walks through the little town on his way to the château, he observes by moonlight that the steps of the vicarage are
covered with cuttings of boxwood and leafy branches of laurel, in
accordance with the rustic custom of decorating thus the threshold of newlyweds on their wedding day. Realizing that this was
an ignoble prank of the village louts to humiliate the priest whose
sister Tota Revaux (whom the reader has already met in *Ce qui
était perdu*) they accused of being Alain's mistress, Gradère responds to a sudden impulse of charity and removes the foliage
before the priest can discover his humiliation on the morrow.

Installed in the château, Gradère watches Andrès sign over his
remaining property to the grasping Desbats, after which the marriage contract between Andrès and Catherine is to be signed.
Catherine, however, refuses her consent (to the great joy of her
father who has now purchased the coveted acres), not because

she does not love Andrès, but because she has learned of his love affair with Tota. Anxious to get rid of the dangerous Gradère whose resentment they fear, old Desbats and Catherine have concocted a conspiracy to bring Aline to the château with her damaging proofs of Gradère's previous misdeeds, which will be sufficient to turn him over to the law. Mathilde, however, learning of the plot, warns Gradère of his danger, and the latter, counterfeiting the voice of Aline, telephones from another town that Aline's arrival will be delayed three days by illness.

Meeting her at the train on her arrival, on the pretext of finding a shortcut to the château, Gradère takes her through the woods to an abandoned sandpit, smothers her to death, buries her in a trench he had dug the day before, and returns to his room feverish and exhausted. When Aline does not arrive from Paris three days later, Desbats, Catherine, and Mathilde accuse Gradère of his crime, but Andrès, still under the charm of the father he admires, is unwilling to believe him guilty. In an effort to reassure his son, Gradère insists that he did not leave the house the night in question; Andrès, knowing this to be a lie, rushes from the room in tragic disillusionment. On Mathilde's suggestion, Gradère goes late at night to confess everything to the priest Alain, who receives him charitably and because of his feverish condition allows him to remain at the vicarage.

In the Epilogue, we learn that four months later Alain has persuaded Gradère not to make a confession at the judicial hearing. Gradère, having avowed all to the priest, is now about to die in the odor of sanctity. At the château, amidst the fragrance of springtime and the distant music of the nightingales Andrès, still heartbroken at the loss of Tota, has found consolation in the love of his cousin Catherine whom he will marry.

As we have so often observed, there is scarcely any novel of Mauriac which has not been preferred to all others by at least one critic, and *Les Anges noirs* is no exception. Thus we find one admirer asserting: "Perfectly balanced, free from any overemphasis, *Les Anges* is indeed the authentic, integral novel which can be placed on the same level as *Le Désert de l'amour*, but surpasses it perhaps in perfection of line and constant equilibrium of structure." [10] Yet several critics, even while finding much to admire in this novel, are perturbed by Mauriac's emphasis on the salvation of the criminal Gradère through a sudden manifestation of Divine

Grace. André Billy is rather representative of this criticism when
he concludes sarcastically: "Be nice, be courteous, make from
time to time an elegant gesture, and then assassinate as much as
you like, you are sure of going to heaven." [11]

While Mauriac has had less success than usual in giving indi-
viduality to his secondary characters—Adila, Mathilde, old Desbats, Catherine, and Andrès—he has achieved a striking contrast
in the two principal figures, the repentant villain Gradère and the
saintly village priest. Gradère indeed is one of the most complicated of Mauriac's protagonists. On the one hand, he is portrayed
as the embodiment of gratuitous evil, employing his physical
charm to corrupt and dominate all those around him, lacking in
remorse for the brutal murder of Aline. Yet he is aware of his own
wicked instincts and capable of flashes of generosity and compassion as shown, for instance, in his removal of the foliage on the
vicarage doorstep to save the priest from degrading mockery, or
in his desperate efforts to retain the respect and affection of his
son. In dramatic contrast, we are confronted with the gentle figure of the young priest Alain, so appealing in his tragic loneliness,
clinging tenaciously to his faith despite the scornful jibes of his
parishioners. Perhaps the most poignant scene in the volume is the
anguish with which Alain contemplates the moribund form of the
repentant criminal whose salvation he has assured, while he himself struggles desperately to control his own doubts and misgivings.

Never perhaps has Mauriac painted a blacker picture of peasant and bourgeois morality, not only in the callous buffoonery of
the village youth, but also in the sordid chicanery and lust for
property exhibited by old Desbats and the other members of his
family. The atmosphere of bickering, hatred, and underhand plotting at the château is powerfully reinforced by references to the
continuous cold fog and rain of autumn. The episode of Aline's
murder is also enhanced in horror by the presence of rain and
wind, the desolate silence of the pine forest, and the ghastly contrast of the sandpit where Gradère had played as a child with little
Adila and Mathilde and its present function as a grave for the
murdered woman. Yet Mauriac in an interview vigorously defended himself against the accusation that this novel is too blackly
pessimistic.

My novels and especially *Les Anges noirs* do not have the accent of despair which certain ones persist in seeking there, since I have resolved the problem of evil by faith and hope. . . . It is a book of hope, its profound meaning is that the most debased, the most guilty individual is capable of being saved.[12]

Indeed the Epilogue forms a sharp contrast with the enveloping gloom which enshrouds the rest of the book. The rebirth of the world in the spring, the fragrance of the lilacs, the tender calls of the nightingales form a fitting ambiance for the restored harmony of the château and the peaceful end of Gradère, watched over by his son, then by the little priest.

In spite of the flaws already mentioned—melodramatic complexity of plot, implausibility of the miraculous conclusion, inconsistencies and lack of vividness in the minor characters—*Les Anges noirs* is nevertheless one of the most poetic, stylistically, of Mauriac's novels. As so often with him, nature is described not for its own sake but in association with character and action, as for example just before Gradère's removal of the shameful foliage at the rectory:

In spite of the fog which rose from the Balion [river] he leaned on the parapet, inclined over this diaphanous mist, attentive to this rippling. The water had an odor; it was not the mud, not the submerged mosses. The water had an almost intangible perfume, which as a child he had already recognized. His impure childhood! And yet that night called forth in him intact forces of kindness, of love.

Seldom has Mauriac employed more striking metaphors: "Mathilde had set in motion that invincible power, like a careless child who has dropped a match, and all of a sudden the forest flames up, the tocsin rings from belfry to belfry, the roads fill up with autos and carriages." When Gradère, feverish and alarmed, feels safe from suspicion thanks to Mathilde's testimony, he regains his assurance: "the reptile under shelter now and warmed again darted forth once more his little head with silver casque above the bed covers." When Andrès first hears the accusation of murder against his father, he leans panting on the balustrade "as when the bull, sword in throat, totters but does not fall." And finally Gradère's exclusion from the family council after they suspect his crime is likened to "those pines affected by a malady that one surrounds

with a ditch so that they will not spread death, so that they will
die alone."

It would be an interesting paradox if this violent and somber
tale, written perhaps as a "mystery serial," should endure because
of its qualities as poetry.

VI   Les Chemins de la mer (*1939*)

This novel (The Unknown Sea) is one of the richest in texture
and most complicated in plot of Mauriac's works. As usual there
can be found at least one critic (Edmond Jaloux, *Nouvelles
Littéraires*, April 2, 1939) to consider it the finest book Mauriac
has written since *Le Baiser au lépreux* and *Le Désert de l'amour*,
preferring it even to *Le Noeud de vipères*. Yet here as so often
Mauriac seems to have wavered between two different themes,
with the result that the novel lacks unity of structure.

Mauriac first intended to call the book *"Mamouria"* to indicate
the destructive effect on character of the passion for money. We
are plunged into the financial catastrophe in the very opening
pages when Mme Costadot, learning that bankruptcy of the broker Oscar Révolou is imminent, comes to demand from her friend
Lucienne Révolou the four hundred thousand francs she has in-
vested. She suggests that Lucienne proceed at once to Oscar's
château south of Bordeaux to avert a possible suicide. On arrival
there the family find their worst fears realized. Oscar, overwhelmed by the crash of his business interests, stricken even more
by the flight of his mistress with the profligate elder son of Mme
Costadot, has put a bullet through his head.

The effects of this disaster are soon evident in both families.
Julien, the elder son of the Révolou family, crushed by the loss of
his social prestige as one of the leading young men of Bordeaux,
obstinately shuts himself up in his room as a perpetual recluse, a
"malade imaginaire," until he dies from a real illness several years
later. Mme Révolou, half-mad with despair, devotes herself entirely to this son, completely unable to cope with the harsh financial position of the family. Rose, aged twenty-two, assuming responsibility for the others despite her heartbreak at the loss of her
fiancé Robert, finds a position as clerk in a bookstore. When Robert, escaping momentarily from his tyrannical mother, resumes his
engagement with Rose, young Denis Révolou, inflamed with jealousy of his beloved sister, works insidiously to break off the affair.

Weak Robert, his ardor cooled by the fact that Rose has lost her fresh beauty and attractive appearance, finally screws up his courage to the point of breaking the engagement. Denis, having failed his examination for the baccalaureate, makes an ignoble compromise with the ambitious overseer Cavailhès, agreeing to marry his ignorant peasant daughter Irène in return for the needed reparations on the château. Pierre Costadet, youngest of the three sons, who at the age of eighteen loves Rose with childlike devotion, bitterly attacks his mother and brother for their abandonment of the girl, takes his share of the inheritance, and plunges, disillusioned in his idealism, into the dissipation of Paris.

At the Olympia music hall he meets Landin, formerly chief clerk of the broker Révolou, whom he like everyone else had always considered the essence of devotion to his employer. On perusing the papers of the dead broker, however, Landin had been shocked to find a notation expressing the deepest hatred for Landin *"l'immonde"* (the unclean) whose very devotion and attention to financial details had left Révolou free for his amorous intrigues and thus had been the indirect cause of his disaster. Horrified by this imputation of evil qualities, Landin had accepted a journalistic appointment in Paris where he had become immersed in underground machinations. After accompanying Landin to his home, Pierre falls into a drunken stupor from which he awakens a day or so later. In the paper he reads the startling news that Landin was mysteriously assassinated and that the police are searching for the young man who had been seen with him at the Olympia and accompanied him home the night of the murder.

Now we can understand the true purport of the author's message, which he extracts from the text to place on the flyleaf of the novel.

The life of most men is a dead-end road and leads to nothing. But others know, from childhood, that they are going to an unknown sea. Already the bitterness of the wind astonishes them, already the taste of salt is upon their lips—until, the last dune having been crossed, this infinite passion buffets them with sand and foam. They have only to bury themselves in it or to retrace their steps.

It is obvious that Mauriac means to imply by this sea the love of God. Nowhere has Mauriac's Jansenism been more evident than in this suggestion of predestination which separates from the flock of the mediocre, immersed in their banal occupations and senseless ambitions, those elect individuals who through suffering and tribulation come to rest finally in the secure haven of divine love. This port is attained by only two characters in the novel. Pierre, deeply shaken by this macabre end of Landin so soon after their encounter, influenced also by the reading of Psichari and of Péguy's *Mystère de la charité de Jeanne d'Arc,* accepts the Christian faith and signs up for three years of military service in Africa. Rose, who in her heartbreak at Robert's desertion had first been consoled by the comfort of Divine Love, but who later had recognized in her hatred of Denis' wife a desire to replace her in the affections of her child, now retraces her steps and makes a home for herself in Bordeaux as a devout Christian.

It must be admitted that the conclusion of the novel is disappointing, for we are left uncertain of the destiny of these two characters, whose conversion seems more conventional than amply motivated. The entire personage of Landin, melodramatic and somewhat allegorical as the incarnation of evil, does not ring true.

On the other hand, the depiction of the financial milieu of the bourgeoisie with its pettiness, unconscious cruelty, and lack of beauty or idealism has seldom been rendered more acutely. There is a tragic grandeur also in the two great scenes which tugs at the readers' heartstrings: first the harrowing episode in which Léonie Costadot informs her unsuspecting friend of her husband's bankruptcy and pitilessly wrings from her the signature which releases her four hundred thousand francs; later the interview, almost unbearable in its cruelty, in which Robert confronts his hapless fiancée with the news of his desertion. The first third of the novel, with the dramatic intensity of the business failure and suicide of M. Révolou, which reminds the reader of the great first act of *Les Corbeaux,* is equal perhaps to the finest pages Mauriac has ever written. In his arraignment of the business world and the coruscating effect on personality of money or the lack of it, we think of Balzac and the *Human Comedy.* And finally in Pierre's poetry, those eloquent verses concerning Cybèle and Atis, we glimpse a reflection of Mauriac's own adolescence, youthful enthusiasm, and love for natural beauty. Only the melodrama of his Mephistophelian Landin, the lack of unity and proportion and the hurried ending, together with the ambivalence of the author's purpose keep this novel from being one of his best.

VII   Le Sagouin (*1951*)

After the publication of *La Pharisienne* in 1941, an entire decade elapsed before the appearance of Mauriac's next novel, *Le Sagouin* (The Weakling). A partial explanation for this gap is of course World War II, but more important is the fact that Mauriac's creative energies during this period were directed almost exclusively to the three dramas which followed the brilliant success of his first play, *Asmodée*, in 1938. His return to fiction appears to have been motivated in part by a request from the review *La Table Ronde* for a new novel. During the war he had been interrupted in his work on a novel, the first forty pages of which had been completed and placed in a drawer. This story, which he had originally planned to center about the mother, Paule, now becomes the tragic tale of little Guillaume (or Gaillou, since during World War I it was considered unfortunate for him to have the same given name as the German Kaiser), for Mauriac became obsessed by the vision of the little lad going to his death.[13] This is the shortest of Mauriac's novels; in fact, it is a novella or novellette, little longer than those included in his two volumes of *récits*, for it covers only seventy-eight pages in the English translation. In its linear simplicity of plot, quiet pathos, and choice of protagonist from the physically afflicted, this story reminds one strongly of Mauriac's first brief masterpiece, *Le Baiser au lépreux*.

Its very brevity has aided Mauriac in creating the mood of doom and inevitable fatality which give an impression of strength and unity scarcely surpassed in his writings. The dark and forbidding manor house filled with the savage bickering of its occupants is surrounded in the dead of winter with sticky red clay fields and leafless branches of the pine trees looming eerily through the fog. We are fascinated by these monsters of hate: Paule, the woman of the middle class who has made the fatal mistake of marrying for prestige the degenerate scion of the aristocracy, Baron Galéas Cernès; his mother, who tortures her with almost sadistic refinement; and the old, vindictive Austrian governess. Our hearts are touched by the pathos of the little lad, backward and unlovely like his degenerate father, yet with a spark of appreciation for beauty which might have been fanned into flame by the Commu-

nist schoolteacher but which is crushed into darkness from which
suicide is the only escape.

Of the three classes of society compressed in this bitter struggle,
not one is spared the savage excoriation of the author. Grandmother Baronne de Cernès preserves the dignity of utterance due
her aristocratic lineage, but underneath her polite formality one
observes a burning contempt for her daughter-in-law and disdain
for the lowly born. The bourgeois mother, Paule, disappointed in
her dream of achieving entrance into the aristocracy, seeks an outlet for her frustration in dominating and torturing her retarded
son, whose very existence is a constant reminder of her disgust for
his pitiful father. The "red" schoolmaster, first moved to compassion by the naïve admiration little Gaillou evinces for his brilliant
son and his fascinating library containing Jules Verne's *Mysterious
Island* and similar marvels, soon reverts to his political ambition
and doctrinaire adhesion to the "class war."

When the bodies of father and son are discovered tightly
clasped together in the deep water of the pond above the dam,
the villagers imagine a touching story of a father who tried in vain
to save his son. We who know better, however, realize that it was
a joint suicide, the only solution which these two equally mis-
shapen and disinherited weaklings have found to escape the misery of their mutual solitude.

VIII   Galigaï (1952)

The title of this gloomy tale is explained by the fact that the
main protagonist, Mme Agathe, governess and chief factotum in
the bourgeois household of the Dubernet family, has received this
nickname from the young lad she pursues so amorously and pos-
sessively, Nicolas Plessac. He has taken this title from the famous
or infamous Leonora Galigaï of the Italian Renaissance, who "to
dominate Marie de Medicis used no other philter than that of
strong souls over weak minds." (According to history she was
later, as the wife of Concini, Maréchal d'Ancre, burned to death
as a sorcerer.) This, however, is not a historical novel but a contemporary portrait of the disintegration of society in the stagnant
little cathedral town near Bordeaux in the Landes, which the author has named Dorthe.

In the household of the fifty-seven-year-old *rentier* Armand Dubernet, we find his ailing wife, his passionate young daughter

Marie, and the instructor-governess Mme d'Agathe (Galigaï). The
latter has descended in the social scale by accepting this position
in order to help support her profligate father of noble birth but
crushed by mortgages on his ancestral estate of Belmonte. Marie
is aided in a love affair by Galigaï, acting as *entremetteuse* or go-
between, with the understanding that Marie's lover, young Gilles
Salone, will use his influence over his bosom friend Nicolas Plessac, to lead the latter to a declaration of marriage for Galigaï,
several years his senior. Anxious to abet the courtship of his
friend, Nicolas grudgingly gives Galigaï some faint hope that he
will marry her in the distant future, convinced as he is that his
mother will never give her consent. To his consternation, however, the strong-willed Amazon, Galigaï, does obtain the mother's
permission by alleging a promise of the Dubernets to lift the
mortgages on the Belmonte estate, provided her father makes
over to her all his rights of possession. Mme Plessac even provides
a family heirloom in the ring which Nicolas reluctantly places on
Galigaï's finger as a pledge of betrothal.

At this time Mme Dubernet is taken to a Bordeaux hospital
mortally ill with cancer, accompanied by her daughter Marie.
Gilles follows them to Bordeaux and, no longer needing the intervention of Galigaï, arranges with impunity a series of rendezvous
with Marie in which the young lovers abandon all restraint in
their passionate union. Nicolas, disillusioned by the desertion of
Gilles and irritated and nauseated by the overpowering pursuit of
Galigaï, finally musters up courage to break his promise of marriage, convinced that he is thereby saving her as well as himself
from a lifetime of anguish. After the death of Mme Dubernet,
Galigaï presides over the funeral dinner, a picture of mute despair, interpreted by the guests as surprising evidence of her grief
at her employer's demise. On the evening of the funeral the young
lovers make the concession of not meeting in person but watching
each other across the little river—which corresponds to the sword
placed between Tristan and Yseult in the medieval romance.

That very evening old Dubernet, alarmed by Galigaï's announcement of departure within a week, offers her his hand in
marriage, and though she does not accept at once we have the
impression that she will do so, if only to hide from the citizens of
Dorthe her rejection by Nicolas. The latter, like so many weak
and dominated individuals, freed from hero worship of his idol,

Gilles, and liberated also from the chains of disgust which had
bound him to Galigaï, breaks at last his childlike dependence on
his mother as he insists for the first time that she give him the keys
so that he may wander at will on the nocturnal road. "Stranger to
himself, detached from any creature, he seated himself on the
parapet, and remained there as if he had given rendezvous to
someone."

It is perhaps fortunate that Mauriac has followed this novel
with a postface in which, anticipating the objections of his Catholic readers, he has endeavored to clarify the inner meaning of the
work. Looking over the proofs of his works for a complete edition,
Mauriac notices that manifestations of Divine Grace seem to
occur in them less frequently as he grows older. In *Galigaï* the
reader must await the last sentence, quoted above, for this manifestation because:

this someone who awaits Nicolas Plessac at the spot where the road
crosses the Leyrot [river] is God. It was necessary that first should
be struck down the idol, Gilles Salone; it was necessary for Nicolas
to detach himself from appearances, and from this false image of himself. Galigaï reveals to him at the same time that flesh is a sorry
thing, that he is capable of ferocity like other men, but that truly
he has never loved anything but God.

What Mauriac has tried to show in this "black painting" is the
world as seen through the opened eyes of Nicolas, "this deformed
humanity, somewhat grimacing into which Grace has not bitten."
It is proof of the temerity and fallibility of contemporaneous criticism that even in the case of *Galigaï* some critics have been lured
into cries of a masterpiece. Thus so keen a writer as René Lalou,
dazzled by the cinematic procedure of the opening passages,
affirms that "the art of M. Mauriac has never been more austere
and more persuasive than in this prelude." [14] And Jean Blanzat
feels that Mauriac's "manner" is found here in perfection. "If the
style, more exact than ever and doubtless more concentrated,
points out this mastery, it is even better seen in the execution and
technique." [15] Affirming that none of his works are "better made,"
Blanzat finds *Galigaï* worthy in all respects of Mauriac's great
works.

Today's reader will, I fear, find this praise incomprehensible.

Mauriac's sureness of psychological touch seems to have deserted him. Mauriac himself assures us that the title of this work might well have been "Desire and Disgust." Instead of the terrifying monsters which people find in some of his greatest works, we meet here only petty gnomes, sunk in mediocrity, consumed with petty jealousies and sordid acquisition of pelf. In the strange infatuation of Nicolas for his comrade Gilles, we would be tempted to observe homosexual undertones, were it not that the author in his postface warns us against this interpretation, asserting that he has only tried to portray "friendship, or rather that intermediate sentiment between friendship and love inspired by a comrade from childhood." The unceasing pursuit of young Nicolas by that amazon-like creature Galigaï is more grotesque than appealing, and the one bright feature lighting up the novel's shadows, the fresh young love between Gilles and Marie, is frankly physical and sexual, with no overtones of nobility or spirituality. Seldom does nature intervene here with its poetry. We are left with the impression of an anachronism—a gothic cathedral surrounded by gray roofs of a town once the seat of an archbishopric but now slowly perishing in a welter of greed and loss of faith. I should have to nominate *Galigaï* indeed, along with *Ce qui était perdu,* as the weakest of Mauriac's mature productions.

IX L'Agneau (*1954*)

According to Mauriac, *L'Agneau* (The Lamb) is not exactly a sequel to *La Pharisienne,* although two of the principal characters in the earlier novel, Jean de Mirbel and Brigitte Pian, reappear here some ten years or so older. To understand the novel it is not absolutely necessary to have read its predecessor, though it is easier to understand Jean's sadistic nature if we recall the tragic disillusionment he underwent in regard to his mother, as related in the earlier volume. Mauriac worked on this book for several years, changing it in its final version because he felt he had concentrated too much attention on the "wolf" (Jean de Mirbel) rather than on the "lamb," Xavier, who now becomes a sort of saint and whose vocation is "to suffer in the place of others and die through and for others." Admitting that he never knew a person exactly like Xavier, Mauriac does not feel that he has invented him, because "I love him in certain beings whom I know, who have the same gifts." [16]

In this the last of his novels, Mauriac has shown an interesting innovation in technique of plot construction, different from the long flashback he had employed with such success in several novels. At the very beginning we have a sort of epilogue in which we hear the conversation between Jean de Mirbel and his wife, both afflicted with remorse for the tragic death of the protagonist, Xavier, as a result of the events to be chronicled in the main body of the novel. From time to time, furthermore, the narrative is interrupted briefly by returns to this dialogue, with its overtones of pity, self-accusation, and conjugal reconciliation. This method may seem almost like a *gageure*, for it risks diminution of interest on the part of the reader, aware from the very outset that Xavier's life will end tragically; yet by almost a paradox our attention is whetted rather than abated as we plunge ahead to discover the circumstances resulting in final catastrophe.

As the story opens we see Xavier, a young man of twenty, seated in a railway coach in Bordeaux, about to leave for Paris to begin his seminary training on the morrow. He observes on the platform the strange behavior of a couple—a young woman obviously full of emotional attachment for her husband about to leave her, the latter indifferent and almost hostile. When Jean de Mirbel enters the same compartment where Xavier is sitting, the young candidate for the priesthood finds himself overcome with curiosity for penetrating souls and, before arriving in Paris, has learned that Jean has deserted his wife. Taking advantage of Xavier's desire to bring about a reconciliation, Jean persuades Xavier to spend the night with him, renounce his plan for entering the seminary, and return with him to his country home in the Landes.

Here Xavier finds that Jean's wife Michèle is accompanied by her aged stepmother, Mme Pian (the protagonist of *La Pharisienne*); the latter's charming young secretary, Dominique; and an adopted child, Roland, whom Michèle had taken from a foundling asylum because of her despair at not having a child by her husband. Mme Pian, whose reformation at the end of the preceding novel has evidently not been permanent, still obsessed by her pious insistence on molding the lives of those around her, accuses Xavier of an illicit relationship with Jean, whose reputation in the neighborhood is shady, to say the least. Learning the romantic infatuation which has apparently sprung up almost overnight between Xavier and her pretty young secretary, she admits to Xavier that perhaps she has misjudged him, then proceeds to whisk Dominique back with her to Bordeaux in order to save this young person from contamination (and of course to keep her under her own domination).

Xavier, heartbroken at this sudden ending of his idyl, nevertheless resolves to remain with the Mirbels if only to protect the helpless waif Roland from the sadistic hate and persecution of Jean, who has resolved to send him back to the orphanage. Though the ill-favored and brutish youngster shows little gratitude for his benefactor, Xavier has drawn up a will leaving him his entire estate of 150,000 francs. He conducts Roland to the *curé* of Baluzac, where he is met by Dominique and placed in the care of a responsible guardian. When Jean discovers that Xavier has arranged Roland's escape, he drives in a rage the three kilometers to Baluzac, encounters Xavier returning on a bicycle borrowed from the priest and, unable to stop his car in time, runs him down and kills him. Such is the tragic end of the frail and generous "lamb," a victim not only of Jean's cruel scheming and of Mme Pian's hypocritical austerity, but also of the *curé* whose materialism and loss of spiritual faith Xavier had tried unsuccessfully to combat.

Yet through the miraculous intervention of Divine Grace this pathetic "lamb," whose life had seemed only a succession of painful defeats, becomes the agent to rekindle the spirit of love in all those around him. Not only does the dull curate feel himself awakened by his recognition that this lad was an authentic saint, and Mme Pian, touched with remorse, have masses for Xavier performed throughout the land, but most important of all, Xavier has achieved the purpose for which he had renounced the seminary, namely the reconciliation of Michèle and Jean, taught by Xavier's example that love and sacrifice can exist on this earth.

It would have been pleasant to say in this discussion of Mauriac's final work in fiction that he had concluded with another masterpiece, that he wrote in the full possession of his powers. Unfortunately, however, the opposite is true. Perhaps because of the very Racinian intensity and concentration of the plot, sufficient time is not afforded to render credible the romantic idyl between Xavier and Dominique. Too obviously, I think, Mauriac has tried to humanize his saint by bringing in this digression of passionate love. Michèle is a somewhat shadowy figure, made concrete only in her coquetry toward Xavier. Jean de Mirbel is a vaguely demonic figure, and we are left somewhat uncertain whether his intervention in the life of Xavier was motivated only by diabolic desire to take a soul away from God or by his penchant for homosexuality. The word itself is never mentioned in the novel, but the innuendoes and suspicions expressed by Brigitte Pian and others, together with our recollection of the strange physical attraction between the two young men in *Galigaï*, leave the reader with the impression that this subject was haunting the author. At any rate, as critics have said, in no novel of Mauriac are Heaven and Hell so intimately blended. The death of Xavier, too, is something of an enigma: Did he in a moment of despair at his apparent failure to save Jean's soul and to revitalize the priest's faith plunge headlong into the approaching car to commit suicide (which he had earlier contemplated but rejected as being incompatible with Christian faith), or was he merely blinded by the headlights as suggested by the civil authorities? And finally, the regeneration of Jean at the end, through the miraculous intervention of Grace, may seem a little unconvincing, despite his very evident remorse and conviction of guilt for Xavier's death.

Why did Mauriac renounce the writing of fiction after the completion of *L'Agneau?* He expressed to this writer his disappointment at the severe reception of this novel by critics, though he added that the response from the general public was excellent. Yet a perusal of contemporaneous criticism would not seem to bear out this explanation. Robert Kanters, for instance, praised the novelist for his audacity in making of a sacerdotal vocation which failed a higher religious vocation and for having introduced into his novelistic universe, beyond figures of priests, a figure of a saint.[17] And another critic contended that "it is of all his works one of the most inspired, one of the truest also; because one of the most mysterious." [18] (Another illustration of the fallibility of contemporaneous criticism, unable to see the forest for the trees.)

The real reasons why Mauriac, after *L'Agneau*, abandoned fiction for his present journalistic activity can be found, I think, in an article "Grève sur le tas" which he wrote for *Le Figaro Littéraire*, August 10, 1958. When I asked him if this article summarized his position adequately,[19] he replied in the affirmative and I therefore list them briefly: lack of sympathy for the type of novels rolling off the presses in such numbers today, inspired by the ridiculous proliferation of literary prizes; the present trend to substitute description of physical objects for the study of the human soul; perhaps also the fact that old age leaves him little time to express his reactions in the lengthy form of novels. "I approach therefore without the intermediary of fiction this history in which I am engaged, which concerns at the same time the nation, the social groups to which I belong, and myself." An even more personal reason to account for Mauriac's abstention was that all his novels were merely an attempt to rediscover "that fragrant and sad world of childhood, the reflection of which is being blotted out little by little and no longer interests anyone."

CHAPTER 5

The Masterpieces

I Le Baiser au lépreux (*1922*)

NO NOVEL of Mauriac fails to repay the reader to some extent, and there are very few which have not been acclaimed by at least one bemused critic as a true masterpiece. Now, however, enough time has perhaps elapsed since his final effort in fiction for a relative agreement or consensus to have been reached to predict that five or six of his novels at least have attained the status of master works in all likelihood destined to endure in the repertoire of French fiction. Interspersed with others of lesser value, these have all been produced within his golden decade from 1922 to 1932, with the exception of that final explosion of genius, *La Pharisienne*, in 1941. The first of these, unheralded by any of his previous attempts in the subjective novel, arrived like a thunderclap with *Le Baiser au lépreux* (A Kiss for the Leper).

Since I have been rather caustic in my remarks concerning the mistakes into which contemporary criticism has often been led by too hasty first impressions, it is only fair to state that, with one notable exception, French critics were able to recognize at once the unusual qualities of this brief work by a hitherto unknown author. Le Cardonnel, for instance, found it a little masterpiece which classed Mauriac among the writers of the very first rank, comparing it to Flaubert's *Un Coeur simple*.

If it is no less perfect in form, it is, however, more human. One feels in it a loving understanding of man rather than that haughty and somewhat stupid scorn of Flaubert's work. It is moreover the most deeply religious story Mauriac has written even though it contains no characters who are constantly praying.[1]

Vandérem and Jaloux share this admiration and François LeGrix finds its greatness in the fact that though the protagonists are essentially Gascon they are at the same time thoroughly representative types of humanity. Praising Mauriac for his choice of a great subject, which he has treated with simplicity, delicacy, and poetic grace, LeGrix adds: "Mauriac is one of the first and of the few in his generation to have introduced this order of grandeur into literature." [2] Only Souday showed himself blind to the beauties of this new novel: "The rumor has been spread that *Le Baiser au lépreux* is a masterpiece. The rumor is false. This little tale is fairly distinguished, but a little ridiculous. . . . Everything about this story seems to me absurd." [3] Seldom has a critic shown greater misunderstanding of a character than Souday in his branding of Jean as an egotist and a fool, his marriage as criminal, and his death anti-Christian.

Jean Peloueyre, a youth of twenty-three, of repulsive ugliness but with a poetic, idealistic soul, leads a solitary, lonely life with his rich, invalid father in a little town surrounded by the forests of Les Landes. In order to keep the inheritance from passing to his grasping and anti-clerical sister, Mme de Cazenave, and her bachelor son Fernand (who are to become the protagonists of Mauriac's next great novel, *Genitrix*), Jean's father conspires with the village priest to arrange a marriage for Jean with the lovely peasant girl, Noémi, whose humble parents are dazzled by the prospect of sudden wealth. Noémi's desperate effort to hide her repulsion for her ugly husband undermines her health and serenity until Jean accepts the priest's advice to go to Paris for a few months, ostensibly to do research in the National Library. Here he leads a pitifully drab and lonesome existence and when he returns, called back by a letter from the priest, Noémi is shocked by his enfeebled state. A handsome young doctor is called in, and it is obvious that Noémi needs all her religious scruples to resist his advances. When Jean observes with sadness that the healthy bloom Noémi had acquired during his absence is fading, he makes the great decision to sacrifice himself, spends all his free time at the bedside of a consumptive friend, and contracts the disease himself. Noémi, overcome with remorse, fills his last days with ardent ministration, but he is tortured by the daily sight of the young doctor and the thought that Noémi may succumb to his seduction after Jean's death. Father Jérôme agrees to leave all his property to Noémi on condition that she will never remarry.

Partly in order not to disappoint her parents' hopes for this inheritance, partly also because she feels obscurely the grandeur of her
renunciation, Noémi enters upon an eternal widowhood.

Never before *Le Baiser au lépreux* had Mauriac presented such
vivid and moving characters, and with such an economy of words.
Our only physical description of Jean's ugliness comes in a few
lines at the beginning of the story.

He was so short that the low glass of the mirror reflected his pitiful
mien, his hollow cheeks, a long nose pointed at the end, red and as
if worn away. . . . His short-clipped hair came forward at a sharp
angle over his already wrinkled forehead; a grimace laid bare his
gums with their decayed teeth.

Yet the painful impression which this wretched soul makes on all
around him is kept constantly before the reader through the author's frequent comparisons of Jean to a wood louse, a bat, a grub,
a nightbird let loose in broad daylight, a bewildered cricket, and
even more through the devastating effect which his presence has
on lovely Noémi. As a natural corollary of his physical uncouth-
ness Jean suffers from a morbid inferiority complex and shyness
which make him seek refuge in the solitude of nature. Yet dormant
under the apparent torpidity of this social outcast is a truly poetic
soul, filled with gentle compassion for the suffering he is causing
Noémi. In his decision that only in death could he free her from
this incubus he rises in his humble fashion to sacrificial grandeur.
As the author summed it up so succinctly: "lo and behold, he who
had lived like a dead man was now dying as if he were reborn."

Though Jean is the central figure, the other characters in this
tragic drama are also etched with vigorous strokes. Noémi the
husky peasant girl, unlettered and with only an instinctive understanding of religion, is extremely moving in her struggle to overcome her repulsion toward Jean and her attraction to the young
doctor; she attains a certain nobility in her final renunciation, even
though the admiration of her fellow citizens and the satisfaction
of her parents may not be entirely absent from her mind. The
priest, too, is a lifelike figure, suave, self-confident, and scheming
in the early part of the novel, later torn with doubts and misgivings at the outcome of the marriage he had arranged. Most striking of all the characterizations, however, is the ironic portrait of

Jean's father Jérôme who reminds us in his egotism and vanity of Molière's *malade imaginaire*. A slave to the remedies with which his suit is always discolored, a tyrant demanding absolute silence during his three-hour siesta, Jérôme has managed to avoid all public appearances such as weddings and funerals—even that of his own wife—by swallowing sleeping tablets and taking to his bed. His monstrous selfishness is shown by his indignation when his son dares to become ill and share Noémi's ministrations as a nurse and when he insists on the clause in his will which keeps Noémi ever faithful to her widowhood.

The great charm of *Le Baiser au lépreux* comes in part from Mauriac's genius for understatement, for poetic suggestion rather than detailed description, which makes many critics think of Racine. At the very outset the torrid atmosphere of the sun-baked town is revealed by the simple lines: "Grasshoppers were crackling around the house. Like a liquid metal, light flowed through the shutters." A little later when Jean went outdoors, "like the water of a pool, the heat opened and closed in about him." More sober in its descriptions of nature than many of Mauriac's novels, *Le Baiser,* nevertheless, by use of subtle images, ever holds before the reader's eye this countryside of balsam and pine. When Jean leaves the village behind him he emerges "on the route still pale, between two black armies of pines which breathed on him their heated breath perfumed by thousands of turpentine pots like censers of this sylvan cathedral." Noémi, too, loved to drive through the forest roads in early spring.

The gorse stained with yellow the thickets of dry ferns. On the oaks the dry leaves quivered, still resisting the warm breath from the South. The quite round mirror of a pond reflected the outstretched trunks of the pines, their tops and the azure sky. On innumerable trees fresh wounds were bleeding and perfumed this day with their burning odor. The song of the cuckoo brought back memories of other springtimes.

It is in large measure this contrast between the placid beauty of the setting with the feverish suffering and pathos of this tragic union which explains the immediate success of this novel with critics and general public alike. In a sense, therefore, *Le Baiser* marks the turning point in Mauriac's career. Though the following

year saw the startling decline evidenced by *Le Fleuve de feu,* the
admirers of the novelists found the justification of their hopes in
the great *Genitrix* of the same year.

II   Genitrix (*1923*)

In his *Le Romancier et ses personnages* Mauriac has explained
the significant role which houses have played in most of his
novels.

I cannot conceive a novel without having present in my mind, in its
tiniest recesses, the house which will be its stage; I need to be familiar
with the most secret paths of the garden and all the countryside
round about. No drama can begin to come alive in my mind unless
I have placed it in the locations where I have lived. I must be able
to follow my characters from room to room. Often their faces remain
indistinct, I know only their silhouettes, but I sniff the moldy odor
of the corridors they traverse, I miss nothing that they feel or hear
at any hour of the day or night when they leave the vestibule and
come out on the flight of steps.[4]

Perhaps Mauriac had *Genitrix* particularly in mind when he wrote
this, for more than any other of his novels this is the story of a
house. We find ourselves enveloped throughout by the atmosphere of this bleak and rambling dwelling which belonged to
Mauriac's own grandfather. It is near the railway station of Langon, rendered more somber and depressing by the screech of the
night express waking the occupants in terror, the odor of coal
smoke which poisons the June night, the vibration which shakes
the whole house and slams the attic door. The environment of this
vast and gloomy dwelling with its two wings—that of the "enemy"
Mathilde and that of Fernand and his mother—the cold and
cheerless dining hall in which mother and son face each other in
bitter hostility and resentment, the kitchen with its warmth which
forms a sort of oasis amid this expanse of frustration, all this is
intimately interwoven with the drama of these repulsive and forbidding characters. It is certain that the association of dwelling
and personages will remain as vividly in the reader's mind as
that of the Vauquer boarding house with the characters of Balzac's *Père Goriot.*

The narrative element in *Genitrix* as in *Le Baiser* is subordi-
nated to the development of character. In the opening pages

we find Mathilde, the young wife of the fifty-year-old Fernand, dying of fever after a miscarriage caused by the neglect of her mother-in-law, Mme Cazenave. In a flashback we learn of the mother's rigid domination of her son, from which he had tried vainly to escape by marrying the young teacher, Mathilde. "You shall not have my son," Felicité Cazenave had shouted during the engagement, and it soon became apparent that she would stop at nothing to frustrate the marriage. Even during the honeymoon Fernand began to regret his disobedience, and shortly after his return he left his bride in the "enemy" wing and returned to his bachelor quarters next to those of his mother.

After the death of Mathilde has filled Felicité with a mixture of guilt and jubilation, Fernand becomes conscious for the first time of his mother's jealous domination. With furious recriminations he turns upon her as being, through criminal neglect, the actual murderer of Mathilde. In a symbolic gesture which his mother understands only too well, he makes his abode in the room of the "enemy," transforming it into a shrine for the bride he has lost. In vain does his mother protest that she had come to visit his wife in the night, only to be dismissed angrily by the moribund Mathilde. Day after day Fernand makes a pilgrimage to the cemetery, cuts out of a family portrait the picture of Mathilde—casting the remainder including his mother's picture into the wastebasket—and then through a final ironic touch changes from violent reproaches to formal politeness toward his mother, with the explanation that he is acting as Mathilde would have wished.

Concerned because of her son's pallor and lack of appetite, Felicité forces herself to eat copiously of rare meat in order to persuade him to do likewise, although she knows she has been forbidden this fare because of her weak heart. She is seized with a stroke, and she dies during the following winter after several months of paralysis in which her only pleasure is to gaze intently on the face of her son.

Now occurs a startling transformation in Fernand's attitude. Feeling himself no longer spied upon by his jealous mother, he realizes his utter dependence on her through the years, loses all tenderness for the memory of Mathilde, and feels himself entirely alone in the world. Closing up Mathilde's room, he seeks refuge in the kitchen with the faithful old servant Marie, who has served three generations of Cazenaves and is his only link with the dead past. Even this solace is disturbed when Marie's daughter, son-in-law, and grandson come like leeches to force themselves on him. In a final desperate outbreak which makes him resemble his terrifying mother, he throws them a hundred-franc note and drives them from the house. Late that night, as he lies shivering and desolate in the cold, deserted dwelling, he hears a rustling in the garden path; soon faithful old Marie is stroking his forehead as she had done in his childhood.

In an article written shortly after the publication of *Genitrix,* one critic declared that this book would be his first choice for the Goncourt Prize that year because of its nobility of lines, its purity of atmosphere, its elevated style:

The adventure which *Genitrix* traces for us is somber, grave, poignant, melancholy. One observes the double subject which Mauriac has chosen: the grasp which the absent ones, the dead, hold on us, then maternal love with its fierce exclusiveness, bordering almost on passion. In Mme Cazenave he has drawn a powerful figure which is unforgettable and of which not a single feature could be altered.[5]

Mme Cazenave is indeed one of those cruel, dominating women of whom Mauriac is to give us so many examples in his novels. Her cold egotism is illustrated by her indifference to her husband's death, her relief at being the sole mistress of the estate, the matter-of-fact manner in which she handled the details of the will. All her devotion is concentrated on her son, whose political career she did not hesitate to ruin in order to protect his delicate health. Up to his age of fifty she has succeeded in keeping him a bachelor by filling his mind with cynicism toward women and permitting his monthly trips to Bordeaux for his liaison with a venal courtesan whom she euphemistically labels his *"habitude."* Angered by his attempt to escape her domination by marrying Mathilde, she carries on a relentless campaign of innuendo and persecution against the luckless bride and cannot help feeling a sense of guilty triumph at Mathilde's miscarriage and death. Yet Mme Cazenave is not quite a monster of wickedness, for we see her capable of self-sacrifice at last when she begins to fear for her son's health in his preoccupation with the memory of Mathilde.

Félicité Cazenave, facing this old man who was her son, for the first time thought of him not as her property that another had stolen and that she had to reconquer with violence. Then her love began to resemble that of other mothers, which demands nothing in exchange for what it gives. In this mute old woman forcing herself to eat, an emotion was unchained in which passion overcome consented at last to abandon its sacred privileges: let him be happy, first of all.

Her sacrifice in taking another helping of *filet mignon* in order to tempt her son to follow her example calls forth from the author the moving reflection, "Martyrdom shows itself not only in the sublime. One can give his life by choosing from all forms of death the very lowest."

Vandérem is less pleased by Mauriac's portrait of Fernand, but I find him equally true to life in his alternate fits of submission and revolt. The extent of his mother's domination is revealed by his having to resort to furtive smoking in the garden and eating forbidden melons behind the hedge. Though he had married Mathilde chiefly to escape this yoke, the sight of her face so peaceful in death makes him realize the opportunity for happiness he had so carelessly thrust aside. "A river freed itself in him from the ice of a boundless winter. He had waited until his fiftieth year to suffer on account of another being." When he abandons his mother because of his regret for his dead wife, Fernand does not really change his character. Even as a child he had felt such need to make Félicité suffer that he used to bump her armchair with his knee until she cried for mercy. Even now "he remained that same little stamping boy she had nourished; he didn't want Mathilde to be dead; death itself did not mitigate his furious demands." Only the death of Mathilde and his realization of his mother's complicity had opened his eyes for the first time to the extent of his subjection. "In this network, in this sticky web which for his protection his mother had woven round him for half a century he was struggling like a great fly held fast." Yet how natural for his mother's death to bring him back to his feeling of dependence on her and to make Mathilde's image grow dim, now that he no longer feels anyone spying on his grief. In the author's bitter comment, "there are some men capable only of loving against someone. What spurs them on toward another is the lamentation of the one they abandon." And Fernand's final display of energy in banishing the parasites from his home, with a fury which made him resemble for a moment his imperious mother, is typical of such weaklings, awakened from their lethargy into violent reaction when pushed too far.

Although the portraits of mother and son overshadow all others, the minor characters also are graphically delineated. If the relatives of Mathilde, Monsieur and Madame Lachassaigne are sardonically caricatured—"They ate and they put money into savings" was the epitaph she composed for them—the aged servant Marie with "a face like a black Virgin" is presented with tender sympathy to form the only note of compassion in this stark tragedy. It may be of interest to remind the reader that the death of Félicité's husband, many years before the events of the story began, paralleled in every detail the death of Mauriac's own agnostic grandfather, even to the fact that the day before his death he had visited the hospital he administered and that his last words were "we are saved by faith."

Mention has already been made of the important role assumed by this vast, gloomy abode in these tragic happenings. Equally felicitous is the use Mauriac makes of nature, not in long descriptive passages, but in poetic flashes which always typify or influence the actions or the inner meditations of the protagonists. Thus, the healing ministrations of the summer night come as a balm for the suffering of the dying Mathilde.

Night was breathing in the leaves. The great trees under the moon were whispering too softly to waken a bird. A wave of fresh, pure wind, coming from the ocean, had flowed over the tops of the countless pine trees, then over the low vines, impregnated with a final balm in the fragrant linden trees of the garden before coming at last to die out on this little, emaciated face.

Fernand keeps vigil beside his dead wife and looks out into the night: "this grassy fragrance, this rustling darkness gave him the idea of a happiness he might have tasted, which he will now never know." When the mother learns that her son has cut out his wife's picture and thrown her own away, her blind fury is enhanced by the searing heat of the summer day. "Suffocating, the mother pushed open the shutters. The noonday sun pressed heavily on the dried-up garden. Between the dusty lawns the sand in the paths had the color of ashes. The panting of a departing train recalled an oppressed breast." Later the relaxation of the torrid summer in the welcome rain is reflected in the changed attitude of mother and son, from hateful silence to polite deference and respect, for "in fiery countries the passions of men are in accord with the violence of the sky, but sometimes grow calm in unison with it."

The greater depth and maturity which Mauriac has achieved with *Genitrix* is attested by the number of philosophic truths with which the novel is studded. Worthy of La Rochefoucauld is the aphorism: "The worst thing about poverty is that it makes us look upon people from the angle of utility so that we seek in them only their value of use to us." It would be difficult to surpass the lapidary succinctness of Mathilde's demise: "She had the sweet death of those who are not loved." And with what eloquence does Mauriac summarize the underlying philosophy of this tragedy:

She [Félicité] was beginning to learn that those absent are always right; they are the ones who do not hinder the work of love. If we look at our life, it seems we have always been separated from those we loved the most; perhaps, to become less dear to us, it was always necessary for an adored one to live at our side. It is those present who are in the wrong.

The only fault which critics have found with *Genitrix* is the almost unbearably stark atmosphere which pervades the book, one of the blackest and grimmest he has ever written; this is relieved only slightly at the end by the return of the faithful servant Marie to console Fernand in his desolate solitude. Yet because of its simplicity of means, grandeur of subject and depth of character portrayal few indeed would dispute the assertion of Jaloux that *Genitrix* placed Mauriac in the first rank of French contemporary writers.[6]

III Le Désert de l'amour (1925)

With the publication of *Le Désert de l'amour* (The Desert of Love) Mauriac showed the full maturity of his talent as a novelist. Equal in tragic intensity to his two earlier masterpieces, this novel is superior in its masterly handling of a broader subject—in this case an entire family—and of a double plot, so closely linked together, however, that a complete sense of unity is achieved. Here, too, we observe an interesting innovation in technique, that of the flashback which Mauriac has used in earlier novels and will repeat with even greater felicity in *Thérèse Desqueyroux*.

At the beginning of the book, Raymond Courrèges, a somewhat cynical and debauched man of thirty-five, recognizes in a Paris bar Maria Cross, a woman for whom he had experienced a violent infatuation some eighteen years before, and whose repulse of his attempted seduction had left in his heart a rancor which no amorous conquest had ever been able to assuage. As Raymond recalls that episode of his youth, the reader is taken back for the greater part of the novel to the events which involved Raymond, his father Dr. Courrèges, and the enigmatic Maria Cross, then a languorous beauty of twenty-six.

Dr. Courrèges, exhausted by his sacrificial devotion to his patients and his laboratory research, lonely in the midst of his materialistic family, had fallen in love with one of his clients, Maria Cross, a widow of doubtful reputation who through financial necessity has become the mistress of a Bordeaux businessman. Unfortunately for the doctor, he has acquired in the eyes of Maria Cross such an aura of admiration and respect that he finds it impossible to reveal his throbbing passion. His son Raymond to whom the doctor vainly tries to communicate his paternal love, is full of the romantic desires of youth. Returning from his studies in Bordeaux he has met on the six o'clock streetcar the mysterious Maria Cross, going home from her daily pilgrimage to the cemetery where her little son is buried. As they become mutually attracted on these trips, Maria Cross discloses her identity and invites the young man to her villa. Thinking him to be a naïve, pure-minded boy, she convinces herself that their relationship will be only a platonic one, imbued with gentle idealism and maternal tenderness. On Raymond's first visit he feels frustrated by this attitude, but next time, conscious perhaps of her reputation and emboldened by the suggestion of a dissolute comrade, he tries to take her by force. Horrified by his sensual brutality, Maria disengages herself from his embrace and insists that he leave her house forever.

On this same day Raymond's father, Dr. Courrèges, after a slight heart attack, has finally yielded to the entreaties of his family and has taken to his bed on a forty-eight-hour water diet. That evening Maria's servant comes for the doctor, stating that Maria Cross has fallen out of the second-floor window and suffered a concussion. Despite the protests of his wife and family, Dr. Courrèges rises from his sickbed to treat the injured woman.

When he leaves her, convalescent and sleeping peacefully, it will be for the last time, since her "protector," M. Larousselle, has rented an apartment for her in Paris.

Now, eighteen years later, we are back in the Paris bar where Raymond is watching Maria with covetous eyes. M. Larousselle leaves her in Raymond's company while he goes to the counter to drink with two Russian girls. Suddenly he falls to the floor from a stroke; Maria calls on Raymond for help, and together they take him in a taxi to his apartment. Remembering that his father is in Paris to attend a medical convention, Raymond summons him by telephone. Reunited for the first time in several years, father and son realize that their rivalry for the love of Maria Cross has been futile for both. The story ends with the unexpected gesture of Raymond's visit to see his father off next morning on the Bordeaux train.

Compared with Mauriac's earlier novels, there are few sustained passages of nature description in *Le Désert*. On the other hand, by frequent touches the author keeps us aware of the sultry atmosphere of summer in the metropolis and suburbs: the scorching heat exuded by the pavements without shade, the parched surface of the shrubs and foliage absorbing avidly the first drops of rain, and particularly the dark clouds carried by the moist wind from the ocean, ready to dissolve in the torrents of a tropical storm. This atmosphere, surcharged with electricity, contributes in no small measure to the intensity of passions evinced by the chief characters, for, as Jaloux has remarked, "there is in this novel a sort of burning and desiccating flame which goes and comes and which consumes everything on its passage." [7]

Aside from the dexterity of technique with which Mauriac weaves together the double plot of the loves of father and son for the same woman, *Le Désert de l'amour* owes its quality of masterpiece primarily to its vividness of characterization. Of its three principal characters, that of Dr. Courrèges stands out unexcelled in the long gallery of Mauriac's personages. To my question whether this figure was modeled on that of his brother, formerly Dean of the School of Medicine of Bordeaux University, Mauriac replied in the negative. The novel was written, it appears, at a time when his son Claude was seriously ill. "Dr. Courrèges was a projection of myself cast far into the future, when a possible misunderstanding might have occurred between Claude and myself."

Mauriac was quick to add that fortunately no such misunderstanding had ever taken place, but that many of the circumstances related in the story had proved amazingly prophetic. I was reminded of the figure of Sylvestre Bonnard, a projection of the author into the future by Anatole France, and Mauriac smilingly agreed with the analogy. Apparently, Mauriac had originally intended to subordinate the character of Dr. Courrèges to that of his son Raymond:

Dr. Courrèges was supposed to be, according to my plan, only an episodic character: the father of the principal hero. Then he ended up invading the whole novel; and whenever I think of this little book, the suffering face of this poor man dominates all the others and survives almost alone from those forgotten pages.[8]

Mauriac's comment in the same essay that "the more alive our characters are, the less submissive to us they are" might serve as a fitting reply to Sartre's later criticism that Mauriac remains in constant control of his protagonists.

We see Dr. Courrèges first as he is reprimanded by his wife for not responding at once to the dinner bell. "The doctor shook his head as if to drive off a fly and opened a magazine. It was not affectation but economy of time in a man who was overworked, whose mind is besieged by solicitudes and who knows the value of a minute." On the long daily drives to Bordeaux together with his son, Dr. Courrèges tries in vain to break the silence and express his paternal tenderness. Nor is much communication possible between father and daughter, ever since the day she had rejected the hand of the doctor's favorite assistant in order to marry the wealthy and arrogant Lieutenant Basque. In the midst of his crowded schedule of visits to patients and of laboratory research, the only joy which brightened the doctor's treadmill was an occasional message from Maria Cross suggesting a rendezvous. But, unable to escape from his perpetual role as elder counselor and venerated friend, conscious of the ravages of time which are only too apparent in his mirror, he resolves to renounce his hopeless passion and try to revive the tenderness which had once existed in his marriage. The failure of this effort, caused by the trivial pettiness and lack of comprehension shown by his wife in their walk through the garden, leaves the reader with a feeling of deep compassion for the doctor. The true nobility of Dr. Courrèges is finally portrayed in his treatment of the beloved Maria at the time of her accident, when he thrusts from his mind all carnal desire to leave only the conscientious ministrations of the physician.

The character of Raymond is in sharp contrast with that of his father. Equally passionate, he has inherited from his profligate grandfather the physical charm attractive to women. Consumed by the restless energy of youth, he is selfish, cynical, avid for domination yet oppressed with timidity because he supposes himself a sort of social pariah among his companions. It is perhaps this very timidity even more than his excess of sensuality which makes him suddenly act like a wild boar in his attempted seduction of Maria. It might seem unlikely to the reader that Raymond should have tried for eighteen years to compensate for this humiliation were it not for the author's suggestion that this event merely strengthened and confirmed Raymond's essential nature. What makes Raymond not merely a blackguard but a truly human and credible character to the reader can be found in the two confrontations with his father. The first of these is the moment when Raymond, furious at his rejection by Maria, is about to defame her before his father, then desists when he realizes for the first time that his father loves her. The second occurs at the very end of the book when, reconciled with his father by the consciousness of their mutual misery in regard to Maria, he surprises the old doctor by going to say farewell at the train.

The last of these principal characters, Maria Cross (notice the apparent symbolism in the name), is perhaps the most difficult to define. She may indeed be, as several critics have said, a rather banal and mediocre person, and Dr. Courrèges was probably correct in thinking she would have been a quiet, virtuous wife if her husband had lived. Her lack of financial resources and the necessity to provide for her little son whom she loved so deeply had been indeed responsible for her unwilling acceptance of the status of mistress to the blatant and philandering Larousselle. Obviously indifferent to physical pleasure and sensitive to the jibes of society concerning her position as a "kept woman," Maria renounces even the luxury of a carriage in favor of the humble streetcar in order to visit her son's grave. Her mixture of indolent languor and romantic idealization keeps her from understanding the true nature of others—the smoldering passion of the doctor or the violent sen-

suality of Raymond whom she had viewed as an innocent child. In
many ways she suffers from the same "desert of love" as do Raymond and Dr. Courrèges, though at the end we infer that her
need for affection has been satisfied by her adoration of Bertrand,
now become her stepson.

Though of course less well developed, each of the minor characters has a distinct personality: Victor Larousselle who marries
Maria at last through the urging of his son Bertrand; daughter
Madeleine and her husband, the crudely materialistic Lieutenant
Basque who meets in World War I a death so much nobler than
his character; grandmother Courrèges; and particularly the doctor's wife. Petty and immersed in household cares as she may be,
tactless and uncomprehending in her reactions to her husband,
she is nonetheless fundamentally kind. This we realize when, despite her pleadings, Dr. Courrèges rises from his sickbed to go to
Maria Cross and afterward finds waiting for him at the gate the
carriage which Mme Courrèges has brought to bring the exhausted man home.

Yet for the reader, as for Mauriac himself, the figure which remains in our mind long after we have finished *Le Desert de l'a-
mour* is that of Dr. Courrèges, so quietly tragic in the frustration
of his love for his wife, for Maria, and perhaps most of all, for his
only son.

IV   Thérèse Desqueyroux (1927)

Just as Stendhal's masterpiece *Le Rouge et le noir* had for its
inception the account of a murder trial, so the origin of *Thérèse
Desqueyroux* can be found in the famous Canaby case, which was
the sensation of Bordeaux in May, 1906.[9] Mauriac recalls his vivid
impression, at the age of eighteen, of a woman between two gen-
darmes in a courtroom on trial for her attempt to poison her
husband. From this trial he retained for his own novel the
falsification of prescriptions and the testimony of the intended
victim in favor of the accused, while changing completely the
character and motivation of the poisoner, who had been actuated
in reality by love for another man. Mauriac's heroine, as will be
seen, is a far more complex individual, for her drama lies in the
fact that she herself does not understand clearly the reasons for
her crime.[10]

If Mauriac had planned to write only a "crime and detection

novel," he could easily have begun or ended his story with a thrilling courtroom scene in which the impending verdict would have
held the reader in frenzied suspense. Since he was primarily interested, however, in the subtle unfolding of his heroine's character,
he eschewed this facile appeal to the emotions and in the opening
chapter shows Thérèse already acquitted, thanks to the complicity
of her husband and the political "pull" of her father. Then, by use
of the flashback technique, he devotes the first two-thirds of the
novel to Thérèse's reflections on the train taking her back through
the pine forests to a confrontation with her husband.

As Thérèse prepares her "confession," her thoughts go back to
her early childhood, her friendship with Anne de Traves, half-
sister of Bernard, her acceptance of marriage with the latter,
partly to unite her pines with his since the instinct for property
was strong in her veins, partly perhaps to achieve a position of
stability as a refuge from her restless desires. But even on her
wedding day she had the sudden impression of imprisonment in a
bourgeois world of convention and banal routine from which
there could be no escape. On her honeymoon, her romantic vi-
sions are dashed by the prosaic sensuality of her husband. About
to return from Paris, Thérèse finds awaiting her three letters from
Anne telling of her ecstatic love for Jean Azévédo, an aristocratic
young Jew whose summer home is located near the Desqueyroux
dwelling at Argelouse. Inflamed by sudden jealousy of this girl
who has found the romance which she had missed, Thérèse ea-
gerly accepts the request from Bernard and his family to break up
this affair, which looms as an obstacle to a *mariage de convenance*
the family are planning for Anne with the wealthy Deguilhem.

Confident that Thérèse will plead her cause, Anne reluctantly
consents to depart on a trip with her mother. In her first interview
with Jean, Thérèse is surprised to learn that he has no intention of
marrying Anne and views the whole affair as an amusing flirta-
tion. He impresses Thérèse with his sophistication and holds out
for her the possibility of escape from the tedium of her existence
here to the wider horizons of a life in Paris. Anne, in despair at
having received no letter from Jean, returns to Argelouse only to
find that he has left for Paris two days before, leaving no address.

Thérèse's daughter Marie is born, but this brings no alleviation
to her feeling of incarceration in the stillness of the pine forest.
Then one day amidst the excitement caused by a forest fire in the

vicinity, Bernard absent-mindedly takes a double dose of the solution of arsenic which his doctor had prescribed for him. He becomes very ill. Actuated at first by curiosity, Thérèse who had
watched his action without warning him of his mistake, after his
recovery decides to double his dose to determine whether his illness had been caused by the arsenic or perhaps by some other
reason. Fascinated by her discovery, she continues to pour drops
into Bernard's glass until finally his condition becomes so terrifying that he is taken by ambulance to a clinic in Bordeaux where
his case is analyzed as arsenic poisoning. When Dr. Pédemay discovers that his prescriptions have been falsified, Thérèse is placed
on trial for attempted murder. In order to avoid a scandal which
would ruin her father's political ambitions and destroy the prospect of Anne's marriage to Deguilhem, both families decide to
save Thérèse, and Bernard himself testifies in her favor.

At this point, the train's arrival at Saint-Clair brings Thérèse's
long reflections to an end; she finds Bernard awaiting her in the
carriage to take her to Argelouse. As she attempts to explain her
motives to Bernard and offers to disappear, she is roughly ordered
to submit to the plan he has devised. She will be barred from the
kitchen and the rest of the house except her room, though she may
roam freely through the woods. On Sundays she will accompany
Bernard to mass in Saint-Clair in order to give the impression that
her family believe in her innocence. Bernard leaves on a two-
month trip, while Thérèse, refusing exercise or solid food, drinking
coffee only because an empty stomach cannot withstand chain-
smoking, becomes emaciated as a wraith. When a letter from Bernard announces his imminent return, together with his promise to
reward Thérèse if she will cooperate in the family's plans for
Anne's engagement to Deguilhem, Thérèse makes an effort to restore her health and lucidity. Her confrontation with Deguilhem
and the family having the desired effect, Bernard escorts her to
freedom in Paris after Anne's wedding, promising to send her
faithfully the income from her pines.

The publication of *Thérèse Desqueyroux* in 1927 was a *succès
de scandale*, for many critics such as Barbusse, Paul Souday, and
Louis-Jean Finot found it horrifying and immoral, and Catholic
commentators like Eugène Charles completely rejected Mauriac's
contention that it was meant to serve as an "indirect apology" for

Christianity. On the other hand, Edmond Jaloux, while wishing for a fuller explanation of Thérèse's motivation, considers the book "Mauriac's Phèdre," superior to its predecessors[11] and John Charpentier, reminded by Thérèse of Emma Bovary and, in her somnambulistic automatism, of Lady Macbeth, finds this book "impregnated with charity and full of a very moving human truthfulness."[12] More recently, as I have mentioned, a literary jury of twelve eminent French critics selected *Thérèse* as one of the twelve best novels of the half century, and it is now considered by many critics to be Mauriac's masterpiece. What are the factors which combine felicitously to merit this appreciation?

First of all, despite the somewhat repelling violence of the action, the novel has a poetic quality unsurpassed in Mauriac's fiction. By transposing the setting of the original Canaby case from Bordeaux to the Landes so familiar to his boyhood, the author has fused the action perfectly with the milieu: the stifling pine forests surrounding the desolate hamlet of Argelouse where in the summer "scarcely had the blinds been open when the light, spurting forth suddenly like a stream of molten metal, seemed to burn the matting." When Anne, heartbroken and emaciated after her disastrous love affair, joins Thérèse in the garden she is represented as more "consumed than any plant in the August afternoon," amidst the "ashes of the *allées,* the dry and crackling meadows, the odor of grilled geraniums." Mauriac's repetition of the word "silence" emphasizes the terrible isolation of this section. "People who do not know this out-of-the-way country do not know what silence is; it encircles the house, as if solidified in this thick mass of forest where nothing lives except sometimes a hooting owl." But if this landscape is depressing in fair weather, how much more so in autumnal fog and rain. "Until December it was necessary to live in darkness. As if the innumerable pines were not sufficient, the uninterrupted downpour multiplied around the somber house its millions of moving bars." The eternity of this deluge which engulfs Thérèse after her sequestration is magnificently evoked by this phrase: "Finally the rain on the tiles, on the splattered window panes, on the deserted field, on a hundred kilometers of heath and marshes, on the last moving dunes, on the Ocean." Even the pines themselves, so loved by Thérèse, seem to conspire to hem her in: "Beyond, a black mass of oaks hid the pine trees;

but their resinous fragrance filled the night; like an enemy army, invisible but close at hand, Thérèse knew that they were encompassing the house."

Even more important as an explanation for the greatness of *Thérèse Desqueyroux*, perhaps, is the fact that its dark heroine is the most fascinating and unforgettable of Mauriac's feminine characters. To a great extent this is because he has put so much of himself into her restless struggle for independence and self-expression. Just as Emma Bovary was chosen by Flaubert to represent his own romantic rebellion against prosaic mediocrity, so Thérèse incarnates for Mauriac his own problem of the late 1920's, his own frustrations and spiritual dilemma. In an article written in 1952, Mauriac insists that Flaubert's statement "Madame Bovary c'est moi" applies to all the great creations of fiction. "I remain more directly united with my work than any of those who have preceded me." [13]

It will be recalled that Mauriac referred to his own boyhood in Bordeaux as "a prodigious individual existence hemmed in without expression, without any possible outlet." Torn between his Jansenist consciousness of sin and his inability to repress entirely the desires of his own passionate nature, Mauriac found his only possible escape a vicarious one in the creation of fictional characters. At the time he was writing *Thérèse* this conflict within himself had reached a paroxysm of intensity, exacerbated by a private crisis involving the continuance of his own marriage, and by the venomous hostility of some Catholic critics who angered him by their attacks on his work as immoral and inimical to Catholic doctrine. Mauriac himself said in an interview: "*Thérèse Desqueyroux* was indeed the novel of revolt. Thérèse's story was my whole drama, it was my cry of protest. . . . And I might say, although I have never thought of poisoning anyone, that Thérèse Desqueyroux was I myself." [14]

Harrowed by confused desires and resolutions, Thérèse even as a young girl was able to state: "I have never known towards what tended this frenzied power in me and outside me; of what it destroyed on its way I was terrified myself." The element of fatality is strong in Thérèse: "Thérèse did not reflect, did not premeditate anything at any moment of her life; no sharp turning: she descended an imperceptible slope, slowly at first, then more rapidly." Why had she consented to marry Bernard? Perhaps a little from the joy of becoming Anne's sister-in-law, but much more because the two thousand hectares of Bernard tempted her. "She had always had a feeling for property in her blood and the thought of dominating a great extent of forest attracted her." But here as elsewhere in her complex nature there is no simple explanation, for "perhaps she sought less in marriage a domination, a possession, than a refuge . . . she wanted to be reassured against she knew not what peril." Never had she known such peace as during her engagement; "what she thought was peace and which was only the half-sleep, the numbness of this reptile in her bosom."

When on her wedding day she heard the heavy church door closed behind her, she suddenly awakened to the meaning of her future. "In the heart of a family she was going to smolder like a secret flame which creeps under the embers, sets on fire a pine tree, then another, then from one to the next creates a forest of torches." Unable to reciprocate Bernard's passion on their honeymoon, nevertheless "as facing a landscape enshrouded in rain we imagine what it would have been in the sunlight, Thérèse discovered sensual pleasure." On her return to Bernard's family, Thérèse felt the horror and despair of a person condemned to live her life out in a barren prison. "The family! . . . her eye fixed, she looked at this cage with its innumerable and living bars, this cage flanked with ears and eyes, where motionless, crouching, her chin on her knees, her arms clasped about her legs, she would wait for death." After the departure of Jean Azévédo who had given her a brief glimpse of the world of freedom she felt herself "penetrate an indefinite tunnel, plunge into a shadow constantly enlarging."

Later in her sequestration after the trial, Thérèse in her thought of suicide considers for a moment taking her child with her to avoid a destiny like her own, then kneels and kisses the tiny hand: "she is surprised at what emerges from the depth of her being, rises to her eyes, burns her cheeks: a few pitiful tears, she who never weeps." The very fact that Thérèse at this point feels herself to be a monster is the best proof that she really is not one, but rather a creature of flesh and blood, caught in the vise of circumstance.

In his discussion of this novel, Professor Peyre writes of Thérèse that Mauriac "presented her with the most precious gift a novelist can make to his heroes; he endowed her with mystery. . . .

Shade plays with light, and half shades with more glaring color
in Thérèse, the most subtle and the most pitiful of Mauriac's oppressed women." [15] Mauriac, asking himself why some characters
achieve a sort of immortality, concludes that, as in the case of
Thérèse, it is because their contour is less definite and they in-
corporate a greater share of mystery, uncertainty, and prob-
ability than do others. "Why did Thérèse want to poison her
husband? This question has had much to do with keeping her
sad shadow alive in our midst." [16] No doubt Mauriac still had
Sartre's criticism in mind when he wrote in 1952: "I have been
reproached for judging my heroes and for playing the role of
God with them. Thérèse on the contrary is the being who escapes
from all judgment, and first of all from her own, terribly free at
every moment and watching her eternal figure outlined at the
slightest gesture she risks." [17]

It is a fascinating task for each reader to try to unravel Thérèse's
motivation for poisoning her husband. The possibility that she
had fallen in love with Jean Azévédo is of course absurd and did
not even occur to Bernard. If he first concluded that she was actuated by the desire to possess his pines, he had dismissed this facile
explanation before the end of the novel. At their final parting in
Paris she makes a valiant effort to analyze her motivation, as much
for herself as for a response to his question. Apparently she had
acted almost unconsciously like a sleepwalker, fascinated by Bernard's absent-mindedness in taking the double dose, impelled at
first by curiosity to learn whether this had caused his first illness.
Far from trying to excuse herself, she suggests that her action
must have been preceded by months of criminal thoughts. Then
remorse for prolonging his suffering made her increase the dose,
as if she were yielding to a frightful duty. Obviously, she is not
serious when she suggests that she did this "to see in your eyes an
uneasiness, a curiosity." Perhaps she is closer to the truth when
she states: "I did not want to play a role, to make gestures, to
deny at every moment a Thérèse who"—although she admits that
this explanation does not quite ring true. If Thérèse herself does
not understand why she committed her crime, most readers may
conclude, however, that in attempting to destroy Bernard it was
not so much hatred for Bernard himself that impelled her as a
despairing effort to escape from the bonds of family, of deadening
routine, of bourgeois cant and futility. In any case there is no

doubt that for the reader, as for Mauriac, this *"Criminelle"* remains nonetheless *"une créature noble,"* who wins our sympathy if not our admiration in her conflict with the sordid mediocrity of bourgeois society around her.

Since Thérèse dominates the book, it is natural enough for most critics to dismiss lightly the other protagonists. Yet if Flaubert succeeded in rendering Emma Bovary's crustacean husband lifelike, Mauriac has succeeded equally in making Bernard—who so easily might have been merely a foil for Thérèse—a creature of flesh and blood. In comparison with Thérèse, of course, he may appear a rather simplified, animalistic creature. With each rereading of the novel, however, I am impressed by the psychological penetration Mauriac has shown for even this secondary personage. Our first impression of Bernard, gained through the eyes of Thérèse in her long revery, is indeed that of a single-track mind, for whom everything is either black or white. "The most precise of men, this Bernard; he classifies all sentiments, isolates them, unaware of that network of gradations, of passages between them." Yet Bernard, even though he "belongs to that blind race, the implacable race of the simple-minded," possesses nevertheless many excellent qualities. Venerated by the tenant farmers for his kindness, he has also "an integrity of mind, a great good faith; he scarcely speaks of what he does not know; he accepts his limits." Like many uncultivated tourists, Bernard was always uneasy when the numbers on pictures did not correspond to those in his *Baedeker* and prided himself on seeing the sights in the shortest possible time. He shows a curious contrast, though a thoroughly human one, between his ardent sensuality and his prudish tendency to be shocked by the spectacle of a music hall. This *"Hippolyte mal léché"* is less interested after all in women than in hunting a hare and even on his honeymoon is anxious to return to "his guns, his dogs, the inn where the Picon grenadine has a taste it does not have elsewhere." He feels a certain pride in the fact that his family calls upon his bride to help them in their efforts to bring Anne back to reason. Incapable of appreciating Thérèse's witticisms, he holds an almost mystic veneration for the sacredness of family ties, and it is this which induces him to avoid punishment for Thérèse in order to keep the family honor intact. Provincial that he is, Bernard nevertheless has had some education: "they said of him that he had gone out of his hole"; Thérèse even congratulated herself on his being a man "with whom conversation was possible."

Yet this man, usually so calm and stoical, was capable of sudden anger and cruelty, as exemplified in his savage treatment of Anne whom he dragged roughly by the wrists to her room before bolting the door. After the discovery of his wife's crime, far from feeling his heart broken, Bernard experienced only a sort of tremulous joy at having escaped catastrophe, a renewed "taste for property, hunting, the automobile, things one eats and drinks, for life, in short." He prided himself on his moderation in regard to Thérèse, was praised by his mother as a saint, and felt in himself a certain grandeur of soul. This smugness was increased by his success in duping the townspeople into believing that his marriage was still intact. A final realistic touch to this portrait occurs in the last chapter wherein Bernard cannot restrain an emotion of sadness in taking leave of Thérèse, losing for a brief moment his cocksureness when he pleads almost plaintively for Thérèse to explain her reasons for poisoning him.

Verisimilitude of character portrayal, tragic intensity of narrative, poetic symbolism of background and atmosphere—all these contribute their share toward making *Thérèse Desqueyroux* a true masterpiece.

V   La Fin de la nuit (*1935*)

The inclusion of *La Fin de la nuit* (The End of the Night) here among Mauriac's masterpieces will surely cause some raised eyebrows among students and critics of his novels, and therefore a few words of explanation are in order. One French critic, shortly after its publication, called it the most powerful and perfect novel Mauriac has written;[18] another stated that, if not his most perfect novel, it was at least the most important psychologically.[19] In view, however, of the fallibility of contemporary enthusiasm which we have noted on several occasions, further justification is required. Although I do not consider *La Fin de la nuit* to be one of Mauriac's greatest novels, *as a whole,* I believe that the first two-thirds of the book are worthy of Mauriac at his best. But the truly compelling reason for treating the novel in this chapter is of course because it forms a conclusion to the earlier *Thérèse* and should be treated in relation to it.

In his preface to this book, Mauriac declares that his intention is not to give a sequel to *Thérèse Desqueyroux* but to paint a portrait of a woman in her decline.

During the ten years in which, tired of living in me, she had been asking to die, I desired this death to be a Christian one; thus I had called this book which did not yet exist "The End of the Night" without knowing how this night would end; the finished work partially disappoints the hope contained in the title.

For the reader surprised by this new descent into hell to which the author drags his heroine, Mauriac explains that she belongs to an earlier time of his life in which she was the witness to a period of distress from which he has now emerged. Yet in this portrait of despair and anguish, Mauriac maintains the essential message that even a creature pursued by inexorable fatality has the power within himself to react positively against this force. If Mauriac interrupts his story before the final pardon of Thérèse and her reconciliation with the peace of God, it is because he had written and torn up these pages since he could not envision the priest who was to receive her confession. This entire preface is of the greatest importance in showing Mauriac's integrity as an author, his unwillingness to force his characters into paths which their own logic makes it unnatural for them to follow.

As the story opens, we have a moving glimpse of Thérèse fifteen years after her crime, at the age of forty-five, isolated from social contacts, suffering from frequent heart attacks, her unbearable loneliness assuaged only by the presence of her faithful servant Anna. Suddenly a ray of hope appears with the arrival of her daughter Marie, now a lovely young woman of seventeen whom she had not seen for three years. Alas, it is not long before Thérèse realizes that Marie's flight from the boredom and constraint of the Landes is motivated not by affection for her mother but by her desire to be near a young student she loves, George Filhot. When Marie learns from her mother the tragic story of her early crime and suspects that this may render her marriage to George impossible, Thérèse with a magnificent effort of the will promises to give her all the fortune she still possesses from her own dowry, since George's parents had been withholding their consent because

Marie did not have the resources needed for the enlargement of their business.

Thérèse goes to George's room, persuades him to reconsider the possibility of marriage with Marie, and invites him to the dinner preceding Marie's return to Saint-Clair. After putting her on the train, George returns for a long conversation with Thérèse and receives permission to call the following evening. This turns out to be the climactic scene of the novel, as George professes his love for Thérèse and the latter, overcome at first by this apparent reprieve from the menace of old age and solitude, summons forth enough courage to dismiss George, making him promise to remain true to Marie as long as he lives.

Frightened by the thought of George's despair and the possibility that he may have committed suicide, Thérèse goes to his hotel room the following morning and learns that he did not return that night. Soon she is joined by George's friend, Mondoux, who shares her apprehension that George may have taken his life. When George finally appears, Thérèse replies to Mondoux's insults with bitter sarcasm, then returns to her apartment, remorseful for having brought dissension and misery to all she has known. Convinced now that everyone is conspiring against her safety, Thérèse becomes delirious and completely out of her mind. Marie, receiving a cold note of dismissal from George, takes the train back to Paris to retrieve her lost love or at least to confound her mother with her apparent treachery. Finding Thérèse desperately ill and a prey to delusions of persecution, Marie takes her back with her to Saint-Clair to be nursed in her old home.

At Christmastime, George returns for the holidays and comes to a final rendezvous which Marie has requested. Learning of the fatal illness of Thérèse, he tells Marie of his deep admiration for her mother and demands an interview with her. Thérèse, who has been restored to sanity on discovering that the potion Marie served her was not poison, places the hands of the two young people together, and we are left with the impression that for good or ill their union will now be effected. Thérèse does not die at the end, but we are left with the impression that a final heart attack cannot be far away.

The reception of *La Fin* by contemporary critics, as I have mentioned, was almost uniformly enthusiastic. Although the preponderance of critical opinion today declines to rate *La Fin* among Mauriac's greatest novels, I have observed that many students prefer it to its forerunner, *Thérèse*. This preference is not entirely without foundation. If Thérèse in the earlier novel remained to some extent a coldly intellectual enigma, here in the anguish and loneliness of her declining years she moves us deeply. Overshadowed by the thought of her crime, which still hangs over her, and separated from her child not by indifference but by her feeling that she had forfeited all maternal rights, Thérèse rises to a moment of grandeur in renouncing all her wealth in an effort to redeem herself by making Marie's marriage possible. Filled with sudden happiness at the unexpected declaration of George's love, conscious nonetheless that she is about to commit another crime by poisoning two more lives, she forces herself to perform the gesture—which Mauriac says gives its meaning to the whole book—of pushing aside the hair covering her ravaged forehead in order to disgust George with her and induce him to return to Marie. If the earlier Thérèse possessed the aura of mystery, this later Thérèse in her passionate struggle to overcome her fatal heredity is among the most subtly delineated and lifelike of Mauriac's protagonists.

Why, then, must *La Fin de la nuit* be omitted from the number of Mauriac's greatest masterpieces? First of all, because the poetry of natural setting is absent in this drama, which takes place for the most part in Paris. More particularly, perhaps, because of the sudden decline in quality in the final third of the volume. Just as the reader, deeply stirred by the conflict in Thérèse between her craving for one last chance for happiness and her frenzied desire to avoid a repetition of her evil influence on others, is about to conclude that Mauriac has written his greatest novel, there ensue the nightmarish complications of the final chapters. That Thérèse could have been so affected by the thought of George's possible suicide or by her remorse for her ignoble humiliation of his friend as to fall under the mad hallucination of police persecution seems absolutely incredible. Equally unlikely and "stagy" appears the final reconciliation of George and Marie as Thérèse joins their hands on her deathbed. We must regretfully conclude that *La Fin*, which comes so close to greatness and contains so many passages of moving tenderness, remains nonetheless imperfect and vitiated by its theatrical ending.

VI   Le Noeud de vipères (1932)

Rivaling *Thérèse Desqueyroux* and *Le Désert de l'amour* in the opinion of most critics for the honor of being chosen Mauriac's greatest novel, *Le Noeud de vipères* (The Knot of Vipers; Vipers' Tangle) is primarily a masterly study in psychology. Almost until the end, a unity of tone is achieved by the portrayal of events through the eyes of its tragic protagonist who stands out in such a pitiless, lurid light that all the other characters exist only in relation to him. Called by Peyre "a King Lear with no Cordelia at his side, a Balzacian miser without the fierce passion for Gold that transfigures Père Grandet," [20] the central character, Louis, is surely one of the immortal personages of twentieth-century fiction.

In regard to the narrative technique of this novel, Mauriac has once more had recourse to the method which served him so well in *Le Désert* and *Thérèse*, though this time with an interesting deviation. The novel is divided into two almost equal parts of which the first consists, not of a diary as some critics have said, but of a long, rambling letter which this sexagenarian is feverishly trying to complete before his death in order that his wife may understand the basis of his hate for her and the children, and the reason he has decided to deprive them of their paternal inheritance. The second half of the book, beginning with Louis's trip to Paris, is indeed a diary recounting his efforts to bring about this vengeance, his failure caused by the cowardice of his accomplice, and the transformation of his character during the last four weeks of his life. The final two letters from his son and granddaughter form a ironic epilogue which makes the author's purpose crystal clear.

As I reread this novel in its original edition, its leaves yellow and crumbling at the touch, this seemed the ideal vehicle to convey the sense of futility, frustration, and bitter hatred which these dusty pages give forth concerning a lifetime of compressed despair. The symbolism of the title may be explained in two ways: the tangle of serpents which coil and uncoil in the heart of the narrator, and the reptilian characters who in the person of his wife, his children, and in-laws spy upon his every move.

Now retired from a brilliant legal career after amassing a huge fortune, ill and friendless, Louis is writing the story of his life for the ultimate edification and humiliation of his wife. After a lonely childhood in which he was convinced that his peasant background and ugly features made conjugal bliss an impossible dream, he had known a few brief months of happiness during his courtship of the aristocratic Isa Fondaudège. Soon after their marriage, however, a casual remark of Isa revealed to him her earlier infatuation with a member of her own class whose family had prevented the marriage because of a hereditary malady.

Without revealing his anguish to her, from this moment he retreats into his shell, all the more so since Isa's preoccupation with the children and her constant fear lest his atheism corrupt their faith tend to drive a wedge between Louis and his family. Throughout these dark years he recalls a few momentary glimpses of light: the little daughter Marie who alone showed him tenderness until her tragic death through a medical mistake; a brief interlude of comradeship with his wife's widowed sister Marinette before her remarriage; and best of all, perhaps, the joy he used to take in the companionship of Marinette's son Luc, a lad of vivacity and tenderness who met his death at the age of eighteen in World War I. During the summer vacations spent at their country home Calèse (in reality Mauriac's own Malagar) there were also moments of friendly contact with the gentle chaplain whose Christian simplicity and warmth formed such a contrast with the cold formalism of the family's religion.

The dramatic climax of the novel is reached when Louis, awakening after the effect of a sleeping potion has worn off, hears his family plotting together, in spite of Isa's protests, to have him declared incompetent before he can manage to defraud them of the inheritance they are so ruthlessly seeking. Louis now relates in his diary his trip to Paris where he seeks out a former mistress and his illegitimate son Robert. To his disgust and horror, this son whom he had never seen resembles Louis in almost every respect except for his lack of will power. Louis arranges a carefully contrived plot to leave all his cash and securities to Robert, but the latter, through fear of prosecution, divulges the whole scheme to Louis's son Hubert and son-in-law Alfred. Through a somewhat melodramatic coincidence Louis follows the three men into the church of Saint-Germain-des-Prés, overhears the treachery, and later upbraids Robert for his double-dealing, leaving him, however, a life annuity larger than he would have received from the family.

Detained in his hotel room by illness, Louis receives only a few days later at the Poste Restante telegrams announcing the grave illness and death of his wife. With scarcely enough strength to take the train to Bordeaux, he arrives barely in time for the funeral, astounds his children by bursting into tears over her coffin, then reproaches them for their chicanery in Paris. Strangely enough, however, his hatred seems suddenly to have left him. To the amazement of his heirs, he now arranges to give them all his property, retaining for himself only the use of Calèse during the remainder of his life, together with a small annuity. Soon afterward his granddaughter Janine escapes from a convalescent home where she had been placed to prevent her from running after her profligate husband Phili and takes refuge at Calèse, where she brightens the last days of Louis, who is starved for human tenderness. When Louis dies a few weeks later, his hand is in the act of tracing a last word in his diary which shows him on the point of conversion. In a letter from Hubert to his sister Geneviève we have the ironic spectacle of this son using his father's letter and diary to justify himself (Hubert) in his efforts against his father, since he is convinced that Louis's apparent change of heart was merely a sign of insanity. But in contrast with the blindness shown by Hubert is the letter from Janine, asking permission to read the diary and testifying to her grandfather's kindness and mystical conversion.

As has been pointed out, the essential greatness of this novel lies primarily in the creation of its central character, Louis, who dominates the book in the same manner that Molière's Harpagon dominates *L'Avare*. Concerning his conception Mauriac wrote: "What is most superficial in him, the great outer lives of his drama, are attached to a precise memory. Nonetheless, except for this point of departure, my protagonist is not only different but at the antipodes of the one who really existed." [21] What Mauriac has put of himself into this figure, in addition to his own hatred for religious hypocrisy and formalism, is the miser's tenderness for his daughter Marie and for his nephew Luc.[22]

"The taste for quarreling is a family inheritance," Louis tells us early in his rambling letter; his own father had been on bad terms with his parents. What renders the miser's suffering all the more poignant is the lucidity which makes it impossible for him to deceive himself for a moment. "I have never experienced any vile emotion without being at once aware of it." From early adolescence he had been aware of being a social misfit, his sensitive nature constantly irritated by his inability to charm others. This inferiority complex is evident in his admission: "My youth was only a long suicide. I hastened to displease on purpose for fear of displeasing naturally." Closely allied to this feeling was his jealousy of the refined manners of his comrades at law school. "To envy beings whom one despises, there is enough in that shameful passion to poison a whole life."

If Louis has a passionate craving for gold it is not, as in the case of Balzac's Grandet, because he takes sensuous delight in fondling it, but because he feels this is his only safeguard against abandonment by his family. Yet Louis admits that he had received this vice from his mother: "I had this passion in my blood." When he had the opportunity of branching out into a successful literary or political career, he resisted this ambition "because I did not wish to give up making lots of money." For fear of being exploited, Louis broke off his incipient love affairs lest he be taken in by feminine wiles. If he restricted himself to visiting houses of prostitution it was because he liked to know in advance exactly what it would cost. Why did Louis always spend his summer vacations with his hated family at Calèse? Merely because he was unwilling to incur the double expense of keeping up two households. No more than his family could Louis understand why Marinette remarried for love, thereby forfeiting seven million francs left by her husband. The servitude of a lifetime was so strong that when Louis went to Paris to dispose of a vast fortune, he lodged in a dismal, shabby boarding house and in the restaurant ordered cheese for dessert, "the most nourishing thing at the cheapest price."

The great advantage which the novelist has over the dramatist is the opportunity to flesh out what on the stage might have been caricature into the rich complexity of a human being. Thus we find Mauriac's miser far more complicated than Molière's Harpagon. There is an interesting distinction to be noted also between Balzac's method and that of Mauriac. Balzac gains credibility with the reader by portraying his monsters such as Grandet first as average human beings, jovial, immersed in family ties, respected and admired by servants and associates so that we are almost unconscious of their glide into monomania and madness. Mauriac, on the other hand, shows us first a Louis by his own admission sordid, despicable, venomous, an object of horror for all who surround him, and then by subtle touches convinces us that even in this dark soul there are flashes of human compassion and glimpses of spirituality. Though Isa accused him wrongly of guilt for Marie's death because she thought it was his frugality which prevented the summoning of a specialist, the grief Louis showed was no less poignant than Isa's; his feeling that Marie's spirit still lived on in him is in sharp contrast with Isa's unchristian despair which could not see beyond corporeal death. Equally touching is his appreciation of Luc's boyish charm and grace, so different from the prosaic dullness of his own children and grandchildren. It is true that he had consented to the employment of the young chaplain Ardouin merely because no lay person would have accepted the post as tutor for the niggardly sum of 150 francs. Yet his action in refusing to dismiss the young ecclesiastic on learning of his earlier disgrace merited the latter's spontaneous tribute: "You are very kind." When Louis was on the verge of seducing Marinette in order to achieve vengeance upon his wife, the sound of Ardouin's footsteps and the memory of his praise caused him such shame that he renounced his evil purpose. When Louis discovers the perfidy of his bastard son, instead of crushing him with righteous indignation he feels only pity for him and leaves him a comfortable annuity. And finally, what keeps Louis from appearing a monster of evil in our eyes is the very frankness with which he stigmatizes his own pettiness—a fundamental honesty which exacerbates his own suffering and which contrasts starkly with the hypocritical religiosity of his family.

What was Mauriac's primary purpose in writing this novel? No author, perhaps, has been more explicit in commenting on his own work, and in this respect *Le Noeud* is no exception.

Le Noeud de vipères is, in appearance, a family drama, but, at bottom, it is the story of a *remontée* [reascension, going back up stream]. I try to go back up the course of a muddy destiny and reach the pure source. The book ends when I have restored to my hero, this son of darkness, his rights to light, to love and, in a word, to God.[23]

To understand the increasing role which religion plays in *Le Noeud*, we should remember that this is the first great novel Mauriac has written since the spiritual crisis ending in his reaffirmation of faith in *Bonheur du chrétien*. Yet herein lies the one point of weakness critics have pointed out in this otherwise perfect masterpiece. Mauriac forgets that it takes longer to go back upstream than to descend, and the sudden change in Louis needs more explanation than the author has provided us. It is true, of course, that Mauriac has artfully prepared the way for Louis's transformation by frequent passages throughout his long letter in which he expressed his longing for a spiritual presence transcending vulgar banality and even admitted that "the Christian temptation torments us." It is true likewise that what he despised with such intensity was not Christianity as such but those who in their daily actions belied the very faith they claimed to possess. "Do not many of them belittle a hope, disfigure a Visage, this Visage, this Face? . . . Isa, is there not in my turpitude an indefinable something which resembles, more than their virtue, the Sign which you worship?"

Nevertheless, the complete reversal of his attitude in regard to his lifelong avarice seems a little breath-taking. Is it sufficient motivation to suggest Louis's discouragement on finding his diabolical maneuver in Paris foiled by the ineptitude of his son Robert? Why would it have been impossible to find some other solution? It was natural enough, of course, for him to reject the thought of squandering his wealth, since forty years of penny clutching made this subterfuge unthinkable. Equally true to character was his dismissal of the idea of charitable bequests, so foreign to his lifetime of acquisitiveness. There remains then as sole explanation for the miser's change of heart his realization that, contrary to all expectations, his wife had preceded him in death. "A perturbation in the stars would not have caused me more surprise than this death, more disquietude." So this painful confession had been all in vain, and Isa would never know the true motive for his actions. If he had only remained at home a reconciliation might have taken place, for she had asked insistently for him on her deathbed. At the sight of the family's tear-stained faces, Louis pronounced almost mechanically the words: "I should have liked so much to accompany her to the end, since I was not able to bid her farewell," and he found to his surprise that tears of sincere anguish came to his eyes. Whether it was because now the whole purpose of his confession had been thwarted or because Isa and the children now appeared to him not as monsters but as poor human creatures, his hatred suddenly left him and he experienced only a desire to divest himself of everything material before death could overtake him. Afterward he felt only an immense relief. "I was always mistaken concerning the object of my desires. We do not know what we desire, we do not love what we think we love."

The peaceful autumn, with its fragrance of grass fires, harmonized with Louis's newfound tranquillity. "We reawaken in full autumn and the grape clusters, on which a little rain catches and glistens, will not find again what rainy August has taken from them. But for us, perhaps, it is never too late. I need to repeat to myself that it is never too late." And indeed one final boon was vouchsafed this lonely old man in the companionship of his granddaughter Janine who had taken refuge with him after the flight of her husband. After the pharisaical letter of Hubert, the concluding letter of Janine shows that she at least had plumbed the sincerity of the old man as he groped his way toward the light. "With all our strength we had turned ourselves toward material goods, while grandfather . . . will you understand that where his treasure was, there his heart was not?"

Since Mauriac himself considered the essential message of his novel to lie in this verification that even in the heart of the most confirmed sinner there is the possibility of spiritual regeneration, our attention has been centered almost exclusively on the psychology of Louis. Nature indeed plays a more subdued role in this novel than in most of its predecessors, either because its peasant-narrator could not be expected to indulge in lyrical effusions or because Mauriac through its very starkness wished to prune away anything that might divert the reader from his analysis of character. Though the scene as usual is laid in Bordeaux and the Landes, the comparative vagueness of milieu aids, moreover, in lending a sense of universality to the theme.

Closely related to the author's main purpose is his flagellation of cant and hypocrisy among the so-called *bien pensant* circles of the Catholic bourgeoisie, approached in ferocity by nothing he had previously written unless perhaps by his early novel *Préséances*. As he remarked on one occasion, the presence of God must be much closer to a self-convinced sinner like Louis than to the whited sepulchers of these religious impostors, frozen in the ritual and routine of traditionalism. Lest anyone misunderstand his attitude, however, Mauriac has lovingly portrayed the pathetic, humble, and sincere figure of the little chaplain, Ardouin (his own favorite as he confided in me).

In spite of the mild criticism I have mentioned in regard to the suddenness of Louis's conversion, I cannot agree with critics like Martin Turnell who find this novel "the first work of his decline." [24] In my opinion Mauriac has achieved here not only one of his greatest novels but also the almost impossible fusion represented by the words "Catholic novel."

VII   La Pharisienne (*1941*)

The last of Mauriac's great novels, *La Pharisienne* (Woman of the Pharisees), was published in the midst of World War II and hence received less immediate attention from critics than the preceding novels. Once more Mauriac has changed his technique of composition: instead of letting us see the story develop through the eyes of the chief protagonist as in *Le Noeud de vipères*, he has used a linear treatment in which the narrator, a young boy at the time, recounts in old age the events with which he was concerned as a more or less passive onlooker. One of Mauriac's longest novels, it disperses its interest to some extent from its central protagonist to include a number of her victims, whose stories are intertwined in a series of complicated events which make a brief summary of the action more difficult than usual with Mauriac.

The narrator Louis, a rather callow and egotistical youth of fourteen, and his sister Michèle, a year his senior, are living with their father and stepmother Brigitte Pian. The latter, as overweening and dominating a personality in her own way as that earlier matriarch Mme Cazenave—"Why have I always been so fascinated by possessive natures such as Mme Cazenave, Coûture and Brigitte Pian?" Mauriac once asked himself—is ambitious to erase from her husband's mind the memory of her cousin, his first wife, whose tragic death had every appearance of a suicide. Conscious of her own piety and rectitude, Brigitte is furious when one of her protégés, her son's teacher, M. Puybaraud, falls in love with another teacher she had taken under her wing. Her vengeance is clearly shown when she deprives him of his position, leaving the young couple financially dependent on her.

Her stepson's best friend, Jean Mirbel, high-strung and impulsive by nature, is placed by his unfeeling uncle and guardian in the care of Father Calou, in the tiny hamlet of Baluzac not far from the country home of Larjuzon where Louis and his family are staying. It is not long before Jean and Michèle fall violently in love, to the great jealousy of Louis who feels himself forsaken. About this time Jean's mother, the aristocratic and beautiful Comtesse de Mirbel, comes to a luncheon at Larjuzon. She accompanies her adoring son back to his home with the priest but forbids him to spend the night with her in the Vallendraut inn where she supposedly had engaged a room. Seized with a desperate longing to be with his mother, Jean slips noiselessly out of the window and rides on his bicycle to the inn, only to learn that his mother had left in an auto with some man for the Hotel Garbet in Balauze. After a painful and exhausting ride Jean reaches the inn and sees the figure of his mother and her lover outlined in the moonlight in the window frame above him. Heartsick from the disclosure that the mother he worshiped had deceived him, Jean falls unconscious by the roadside, to be rescued a few hours later by Abbé Calou. A long illness ensues, during which Jean is tended devotedly by the priest as if he were his own flesh and blood.

In the meantime, Brigitte has discovered the love idyl of Jean and Michèle, which she decides to break up for the greater glory of God and the preservation of her stepdaughter. No further communication is allowed between her children and the convalescing Jean. Michèle is bundled off to a Catholic school where she will be under strict supervision. When Abbé Calou, worried by the despair and suffering of his ward, arranges to have Michèle send news of herself to him, the inclusion of a letter to Jean is detected by one of the nuns, with the result that Brigitte in her anger launches a campaign to disgrace Father Calou in the eyes of the church. Jean, convinced that his situation is hopeless by his mother's treachery, Michèle's apparent desertion, and his own failure in an examination, breaks open the priest's strongbox and elopes with the pharmacist's wife, twenty years his senior, who had been planning his seduction in order to take revenge upon the priest she hated.

Now a series of catastrophes begins to open Brigitte's eyes to the misery she has caused by her attempt to play God with those around her. Her husband whom she had abandoned in their country estate, having found in a drawer an incriminating letter of his first wife which Brigitte had placed there for him, drinks himself to death. M. Puybaraud's wife dies in childbirth amidst the wretched penury to which Brigitte had reduced them. Father Calou has been deprived of his parish and exiled to his family home.

Gradually Brigitte realizes that her past conduct has been motivated by egotistic pride of domination; she humbles herself by confessing her arrogance to the disgraced priest. In an effort to make amends, she tries to bring about the priest's rehabilitation and consents to the engagement of Jean Mirbel and Michèle. By a curiously ironic twist, she whose reprobation of physical love had been so austere, develops in her later years a passion for her Protestant doctor, whose accidental death leaves her nonetheless in a sort of mystical communion with his ever-present spirit.

It is not difficult to understand why most critics, though recognizing the great importance of this novel, still rank it not quite on a par with *Genitrix, Le Désert de l'amour, Thérèse Desqueyroux,* and *Le Noeud de vipères.* For one thing, the sense of unity is lost somewhat as we follow the stories of so many leading characters, which interrupt and succeed one another. From a technical standpoint, the narrator's effort to render plausible, by his frequent mention of diaries and letters, the events which he himself did not witness, becomes tiresome at times. For the non-Catholic reader, too, the author's insistence on matters of dogma and theology tends occasionally to weaken interest in the narrative. Finally, although the catastrophes are not melodramatic or improbable in themselves, their concentration one upon another to bring about Brigitte's reformation has a certain air of artificiality which makes one suspect a *deus ex machina* at work.

Nevertheless, *La Pharisienne* is a strong novel, not far from being a true masterpiece. Seldom has Mauriac presented us with more lifelike characters. If the tragic fate of that awkward and ill-favored couple, M. Puybaraud and his wife, partakes to some extent of the sentimental pathos of a Daudet or a Dickens, the love idyl between Michèle and Jean has the freshness and spontaneity of adolescence. Nelly Cormeau is probably correct when she calls the gentle portrait of Father Calou the most moving and complete of all the priests in Mauriac's fiction.[25] Robichon exaggerates, certainly, when he claims that Louis, the youthful raconteur, is not far from being the principal protagonist of the novel and that "it is less a life of Brigitte Pian that he relates than his own." [26] In the eyes of Mauriac as in that of most readers, Brigitte herself is the character who dominates the book, just as she dominates the lives of all around her.

It is not fair to call her "a feminine Tartuffe," for her every move is made through a sincere desire to achieve sainthood. Her physical appearance is entirely in keeping with her personality.

In spite of the heat she wore a high-necked dress with a lace collar that swathed her to the ears. Her large face, with its heavy, lusterless cheeks, was surmounted by a mass of hair puffed out with curls and kept in place by an almost invisible net. Her black, staring eyes had a hard look, but her mouth was always smiling, though she scarcely ever opened it wide enough to show her long, yellow teeth, which were generously filled with gold and stood out firmly from the gums. A double chin gave her an air of dignity which was accentuated by the way she carried her head, by the way she walked, and by her deep voice which was never heard to better advantage than when she was engaged in issuing orders.

The reader is given subtly to suspect a certain sexual imbalance in Brigitte's nature from the very violence of her condemnation of carnal love—a suspicion which perhaps finds its justification in her infatuation with the elderly doctor in her declining years. Her obsession for manipulating the lives of others is expressed in Louis's remark: "She was tasting the pleasure that belongs of right to God alone; the pleasure of knowing to the full the destiny of someone who thought she was imparting a piece of unsuspected news; of feeling that it was in her power to mold that destiny as she wished." Yet if she enjoyed humiliating her fellow man it was partly so that she might have the opportunity to compensate for this a moment later. "Whenever my stepmother had cast a fellow human creature into the depths of affliction, it then gave her pleasure to raise the victim by an act of mercy."

Brigitte was accustomed to being misunderstood and added every instance of this sort to her claims of martyrdom.

Instead of frankly admitting her fault and sitting in sackcloth and ashes, she turned the other cheek, protesting that it was well she should be thus misunderstood and vilified. In this way she added another link of mail to the armor of perfection and merit in which she went clad from head to foot.

She had an uncanny ability to exercise self-control over grievances, waiting sometimes for weeks before digging them up when the offender had already forgotten them. Much addicted to self-analysis, when troubled by her realization that thought of disaster to Michèle gave her pleasure rather than shame, she tried by force of logic to make her pleasure seem legitimate. That she had a sense of pity, however, is shown by her reluctance to let her husband find the damaging letter from his first wife so long as Brigitte was successful in controlling him. When she realized at times the spiritual aridity in her relations with God, she assumed that this was "a sign that she had long ago emerged from those lower regions of the spiritual life where fervor is usually suspect." It did not occur to her "that she had never approached her Master save with the object of calling His attention to her own remarkable progress along the Way, and suggesting that He give special attention to her singular merits."

Even when the realization of her sin was finally vouchsafed her, the pharisee in her did not die completely. "She took pride in the very clarity of mind which enabled her to sit in judgment upon herself and condemn her own conduct. She did not believe there were many instances of a Christian woman capable at fifty of realizing that her feet had been set on the wrong road." Yet whether in her later years she was moved by the gentle sweetness of Father Calou dying in her arms, or by her autumnal tenderness for Dr. Gellis, at any rate this vain woman felt her heart melting at last.

In the evening of her life Brigitte Pian had come to the knowledge that it is useless to play the part of a proud servitor eager to impress his master by a show of readiness to repay his debts to the last farthing. It had been revealed to her that our Father does not ask us to give a scrupulous account of whatever merits we may claim. She understood at last that it is not our deserts that matter but our love.

Brigitte Pian is one of the great characters of Mauriac's novels and indeed of all contemporary fiction. It was Mauriac's opinion as we have seen, that the impression made by this novel in Protestant Scandinavia was primarily responsible for his selection as Nobel laureate a few years later.

CHAPTER 6

The Short Stories

I   Trois Récits (*1929*)

SINCE Mauriac's most successful novels are brief or at least of
medium length, it might be expected that he would find the
genre of novella or *récit* appropriate to his type of composition.
He has produced, however, only two volumes of short stories,
Trois Récits (Three Tales) and *Plongées*. None of the first volume appear likely to add appreciably to his reputation in fiction.
The first two tales in the earlier collection, "Coups de couteau"
and "Un Homme de lettres" are so similar in plot that it is difficult
not to confuse them in our memory.

"Coups de couteau" (Knife Blows) is less a story than the reci-
tal by a painter to his wife of his amorous desires and frustrations
in regard to a young woman he had befriended and protected.
Never, perhaps, has the author's irony shown itself more acerbic,
never has he illustrated more convincingly his theory of the im-
possibility for two souls to understand and penetrate each other.
Unable to comprehend why his confession of love for another and
younger woman should distress the quiet serenity of his "patient
Griselda" wife, the famous artist expresses his despair at being ap-
preciated only through gratitude for his professional aid instead
of having his passion reciprocated. In his preface Mauriac wonders if he has succeeded in rendering acceptable to the reader
such "*muflerie*" [boorishness] on the part of the artist-husband. A
short quotation, chosen almost at random, should suffice to prove
that for most readers the author has not succeeded. When Louis
observes to his delighted surprise that his wife has actually felt
jealousy of the other woman:

—You have then suffered a little, my poor Babeth? He repeated,
"you have suffered" with a vague pleasure. Then:

—Andrée, *she* doesn't suffer. I have never had that happiness to see her suffer because of me. Yet nothing can be as reassuring as the tears of the other.

When at the end of "Coups de couteau" we witness the artist's joy at the telephone call from Andrée expressing her desire to see him again, we note the irony of his realization that her real purpose was only to confide in him the anguish another had caused her. The tragic misunderstanding of these tortured souls comes full circle in the denouement.

"He began to walk back and forth in the studio, repeating one by one each word of Andrée, until he had extracted from them all the poison that was necessary for him to suffer."

The second story in this collection, "Un Homme de lettres," differs from the first only in that its hero (or anti-hero) is an author rather than a painter, and its *souffre-douleur* or victim is not a wife but a faithful mistress of fifteen years' standing. Deserted by the man whose career she had worshiped, she is tortured primarily by the question of why Jérôme had abandoned her for an older woman with sickly children. She urges Mauriac to find out from Jérôme the answer to this mystery. The latter tells his friend that it is precisely because Gabrielle has surrounded him with such tranquillity and isolation from worldly cares, whereas it is in the confusion of a household filled with noisy children that he finds inspiration for his work. Apparently, however, the man of letters does not follow his own prescription, for some days after this conversation Mauriac receives a letter of gratitude from Gabrielle, thanking him for being the agent who brought about Jérôme's decision to put his second mistress with her children on the train to a health resort so that he could return to her. Lest we assume the permanence of this happy ending however, we read between the lines in the concluding sentence that Jérôme has already found another mistress. "The raised hand of Jérôme stopped a cab driver; but I could not hear the address which he gave in a low voice."

In these two stories of Parisian life the reader's lack of emotional involvement is due in part to the unsympathetic nature of the principal protagonists, in part perhaps because, like La Bruyère and the seventeenth-century moralists, Mauriac has given us abstractions, typical portraits of *the* artist, *the* man of letters. The third story, "Le Demon de la connaissance," however, is more effective, not only because it is full of personal memories of Mauriac's own boyhood and Bordeaux background, but also because its young hero moves us deeply in his solitude and quest for perfection. While critics have reproached Mauriac for not giving a portrait of a pure intellectual, he tells us in his preface that this is exactly why he called this story the demon of knowledge: "a mind invaded, troubled, blinded by the exhalations of his blood, that is what one must seek in my sad hero."

In the opening pages with their depiction of the school days of young Maryan, viewed askance by the masters and proctors for his dreamy eccentricities and inability to conform to the rigid rules of the establishment, we may glimpse, no doubt, memories of Mauriac's own rather solitary childhood. Overcome with distaste and repulsion for an active career in the prosaic business world of his family, and attracted perhaps by the opportunity for solitude and the pursuit of knowledge, young Maryan chooses the quiet and austere cell of a seminary. After a few months, however, his independence of thought and his pursuit of new truths render him suspect to the pious fathers, who show him the door.

He arranges with his friend Lange to spend Easter vacation at the estate of his sister-in-law Mone, a confirmed invalid whose husband Robert visits her occasionally on weekends. Despite the chilly rain outside, Maryan rambles through the countryside, leaving his friend alone with Mone by the fireside. Climbing the stairs to the belfry of an almost abandoned church, he encounters a pair of lovers in passionate embrace. Returning to Mone's dwelling he sees through the window a pantomime in which Mone is obviously describing to his friend an attempt that Maryan, in a fit of youthful passion, had once made to embrace her. Furious at what he considers a betrayal, Maryan quarrels with his friend, who then decides to leave on the next morning's train.

When a letter arrives on the morrow announcing Robert's arrival for the weekend, the sudden joy which lights up Mone's pallid face convinces Maryan of his unimportance in her life. Yes, it must be true as Lange had so tactlessly told him, that he was destined never to inspire love. Heartsick at the collapse of his amorous ambitions, discouraged by his consciousness that his search for God had been in vain, Maryan climbs once more to the top of the belfry, thinking of suicide to escape this world full only of emptiness. Suddenly, however, he sees resplendent before him a celestial Face; he feels that he is loved and that he is no longer alone.

As epilogue, the last sentence in the story suggests the ultimate fate of this young seeker after God: "He did not see in his mind that trench in the earth, where, a few seconds before the attack, a few minutes before being struck down, he would repeat in a medium voice the most beautiful words that the war has inspired in a man about to die: 'At last! I am going to know.'"

II   Plongées (1938)

"Thérèse must be your favorite character, M. Mauriac, since you have made her the heroine in four of your works, besides her brief appearance in Destins." "No," he answered this writer, "but I feel such immense pity for her." The two short stories concerning Thérèse were written in 1933 and are the first two tales included in Mauriac's second volume of short stories which appeared five years later. In his preface, Mauriac states that he has written these two plongées into the obscure period of her life in answer to those who have questioned him about her fate. In "Thérèse chez le docteur" some ten or eleven years have elapsed since the end of Thérèse Desqueyroux. Thérèse calls late at night upon a psychiatrist, Dr. Schwartz, in a despairing effort to receive guidance concerning a crisis she is facing. Haggard and distraught, she relates her bohemian existence in the night life of Paris, her unhappy liaison with Jean Azévédo—whom we remember for his role of catalyst for her revolt in the novel—and her present anguished efforts to retain the affections of Phili. The latter, a sordid wastrel in the toils of some financial imbroglio, has returned to Thérèse in hopes of pecuniary aid from her estate; and in default of this, having learned of her early crime, he wants her assistance in poisoning his blackmailer. When Dr. Schwartz greets this confession with scornful laughter and cynically advises her to get what she wants from Phili without acceding to his demands, Thérèse in disgust makes a movement toward her purse which the doctor, terrified, misinterprets as a gesture toward a revolver. At his frightened outcry his wife rushes in, convinced now of his shallow cynicism and cowardice, and compassionately conducts the disillusioned Thérèse to the elevator.

The second of these short stories, "Thérèse à l'hotel," takes place a few months later. Recounted in the first person by Thérèse herself, this brief anecdote shows us a Thérèse temporarily calmed by the suicide of Phili but depressed by the ravages of time which show only too clearly in her mirror. A strange rebirth of hope and tenderness surges forth in her heart as she observes the passionate gaze of a youth of eighteen resting upon her. Through a bit of feminine strategy she engages him in conversation and arranges a rendezvous for that evening. Before she can commit herself, however, she discovers that the young man's interest in her is purely spiritual and humanitarian, for he has seen in this middle-aged woman a fallen creature, a brand he would pluck from the burning. Furious at herself, even more furious with this "poor fool," Thérèse leaves in a rage to mourn the destruction of her illusions.

One critic at least found these incarnations of Thérèse possessed of more truth and carnal consistency than the earlier one.[1] André Thérive was closer to recent critical evaluation in finding "Thérèse chez le docteur" melodramatic and unconvincing, as is usual when Mauriac tries to describe the fleshpots of Paris.[2] In any case we have here a preparation for the appearance of Thérèse in *La Fin de la nuit*. Marked by Parisian dissipation and by the approach of middle age, Thérèse has become a truly pitiable personage, preserved by her intelligence from the depths of moral degradation but speaking now with an accent of coarseness and cynicism, still the prisoner of the crime committed so many years before. As pure narrative "Thérèse chez le docteur" is perhaps superior for the intensity with which it grips the reader, but for irony and pathos "Thérèse à l'hotel" is not entirely lacking in merit.

"Insomnie," written in 1927 as Mauriac tells us in the foreword to this volume, is less a short story than a *plongée* or descent "into the thickness of a life." According to the author,

It is the chapter of a novel that I have not written, for which "Coups de couteau" might perhaps have been the prologue. Many destinies which are dramatic do not furnish material for a novel, because they lack events. The history of the hero of "Insomnie" can have only a chapter. His sorrow loses itself in the sand.

Louis (the same name as that of the hero in "Coups de couteau," likewise a painter and therefore perhaps the same individual), furious at the conduct of his mistress who seems more interested in his comrades than in him, flees unceremoniously to his hotel room, hoping to escape his jealous torments through the medium of sleep. Alas, his vivid imagination forces him to toss restlessly until dawn, creating vivid pictures of his mistress in the company of a rival. He waits anxiously for the sound of the elevator which might betoken her arrival to console him, decides to break off future relations in order to allow his deep wounds to heal with time, then realizes that this solution is impossible since his fickle mistress has the rare faculty of knowing just how far she can push him before reopening his wound with protestations of tenderness. Just as we saw in "Coups de couteau," a masterly analysis of masculine treachery, so in "Insomnie" we perceive the sharp scalpel of the author probing the depths of masculine jealousy and despair.

"Le Rang" (Rank), unlike its predecessor, is a well-constructed tale, perhaps the most successful of Mauriac's short stories. In Bordeaux or one of its suburbs, old Auguste Duprouy who has returned to the empty house after conducting the body of his sister Emma to the family vault in Langoiran where repose the remains of his father, mother, and sister Eudoxie, receives a visit of condolence from his cousin, Hector Bellade. In the act of relating calmly to Hector the tragic account of his life of frustration, he suddenly collapses in a faint. Hector, after seeking vainly any vestige of food or drink in the gloomy mansion, realizes that the old man is a victim of hunger. He takes him to a restaurant where, his vitality restored, Auguste proceeds to finish his sad tale.

His father's dying words had implored his mother to maintain her position in society at no matter what cost. This implacable old lady, who reminds us of the grim figure of Mme Cazenave in *Genitrix*, exerts a dominating role in control of the household. First she refuses to allow Emma and Eudoxie to give singing or piano lessons, since this would be considered retrogression from their social standard of respectability and decorum. Then she forces her

son Auguste to renounce a brilliant career as scholar and teacher
to accept a lucrative offer as traveling salesman for the great wine
firm of Harry Maucoudinat. A final straw, which effectively
breaks the back of Auguste's independence, is his mother's refusal
to allow his marriage to the woman he loves, since this would
entail the removal of mother and old-maid sisters to a comfortable
nursing home.

Some months after this conversation it is discovered that Auguste had died alone in the desolate mansion three days before
the neighbors found his emaciated corpse. Hector is deeply moved
by the contrast with the radiant youth he had known in his childhood. A final ironic touch is afforded by his wife's decision, despite the heavy expense, to have the body transported to the family funeral vault at Langoiran. "He would have been pleased, poor
old Auguste, if he had been able to foresee that he would rejoin
his mother, Eudoxie, Emma for eternity." Hector asked, "Do you
think so?"

In this mordant flagellation of pride and social prestige among
the upper bourgeoisie Mauriac has returned to the theme of his
early novel *Préséances* (in which the name of Harry Maucoudinat
was also prominent).

A refreshing contrast to this stark tale of genteel poverty and
bourgeois pride is the final "Conte de Noël" or "Christmas Story"
which concludes the volume, with its delicate fragrance and nos-
talgic charm of Mauriac's own childhood in Bordeaux. As his
seven-year-old comrades gather at the school preparatory to
dismissal for the Christmas holidays, the overgrown bully Cam-
pagne jeers at little Jean de Blaye with his long silken tresses
(which remind young Frontenac of little Lord Fauntleroy) and
mocks his naïve belief that it is the little Jesus who descends in the
chimney to fill his shoes with presents. Since his mother has told
him this, Jean insists that it must be true, for his mother never lies.
Nevertheless, Frontenac, whose skepticism has been aroused, persuades Jean to stay awake also on Christmas Eve in order to discover the truth. Little Frontenac does indeed perceive that it is his
mother who performs this function, thinking him safely asleep,
yet somehow he is not disillusioned for he feels in his mother the
spirit of the Christ child.

On returning to school after New Year's Day, Frontenac finds a

new Jean de Blaye, shorn of his curly locks, shorn also of his childlike faith. Their tender companionship has been broken, and since
Jean's family soon leaves Bordeaux, Frontenac loses all contact
with his chum. Many years later, when Frontenac (Mauriac) is a
student in Paris celebrating Christmas Eve in a noisy bar, he encounters a youth whom he mistakes at first for Jean de Blaye, but
who turns out to be his younger brother, Philippe. The latter tells
him how Jean had been disillusioned, first by learning it was his
mother after all who placed the presents, later that the family
treasure box contained only his shorn locks, as if his mother
wished always to keep him in her mind as a child. As he matured,
little Jean had fallen into vice, and the last word they had received was of his death in a hospital in Saigon.

As Mauriac returned to his room, in spite of his desire for sleep
he decided to write down this story of little Jean de Blaye. Creating in his imagination the details which led from that moment of
disenchantment to Jean's death, after a misspent youth, in a Saigon hospital, "it is that night that I became a novelist, or at least
that I became conscious of this power. . . . A novelist had just
been born and was opening his eyes upon this sad world."

CHAPTER 7

Mauriac's Theater

I Asmodée (*1938*)

AS DORIVAL suggested, Mauriac was bound some day to approach the theater, which is the perfect form of the seventeenth-century classicism he admires so much.

He is the only one of our writers today to write books of pure psychology, just like La Rochefoucauld and La Bruyère. He shares with the moralists of the seventeenth century an ardent interest in human passions. Like them also he chooses a crisis in his novels, breaking with the nineteenth century as found in *Madame Bovary*. Mauriac is as far removed from the *roman fleuve* as is Racine.[1]

Like many other novelists, Mauriac had long been tempted by the stage, since he realized that the novelist and the dramatist had the same purpose in common, namely "to invent beings who give the reader and the spectator the illusion of life." If he had not attempted the theater earlier, it was because he feared the technical difficulties, the long periods of waiting, the necessity of breaking into what for him was an unknown world. In the magazine *Conférencia* Mauriac tells us the fortuitous incident which finally broke down his resistance.[2] In 1937 a performance of *Don Juan*, sung by Ezio Pinza and conducted by Bruno Walter at the Festival of Salzburg had awakened in him an impatient desire to see his own characters live and suffer on the stage. Lunching at Maxim's with his friend Bourdet who had recently become administrator of the Théâtre Français, he assured Bourdet that he was incapable of imagining a plot for the theater. "I have only characters" he said, thinking in particular of the one who was to become M. Coûture of his first play. "You have characters," Bourdet replied "Why then, everything is fine; that's the only thing that matters; your play is made." Mauriac was frank to confess that he

owed the success of *Asmodée* to the intelligent counsels of Bourdet, who had him rewrite it many times in order to concentrate
the principal attention on his leading protagonist, Blaise Coûture.

Influenced no doubt by the opinion of critics who maintained
that his novels owed their success primarily to their poetic atmosphere, Mauriac was careful to carry over into *Asmodée* the ambiance of his novels, as we learn in the *Conférencia* article.

I yielded to the temptation of gratifying myself by reconstituting on
the stage of the Théâtre Français the climate of my vacations in days
gone by, the moonlight over the pine trees, the airs my brothers and
I used to sing on hot summer evenings while seeking the stars between the tree tops. I insisted that the children in my play sing a
certain aria from *Cinq Mars*, a forgotten opera of Gounod, "Nuit
resplendissante et silencieuse" because it was the one we used to sing
fifty years ago when before going to bed we took a last turn in the
park.

Mauriac has himself explained how the title and subject matter
of *Asmodée* first came to him. As he was crossing France in a train
an English lady in his compartment had said to him: "Maître,
when I glimpse through the portières these old bourgeois dwellings, the trees in groups of five, the carefully trimmed arbors, I
imagine all sorts of dramas behind these closed shutters, under
these tile or slate roofs." From this remark Mauriac was reminded
of Asmodée "the limping devil who in Lesage's novel raises the
roofs of houses." Thus when Marcelle in the play asks the visiting
English lad, Harry, why he had chosen to come to this out-of-the-
way section of France in the Landes, he replies that on his many
trips across France with his father, an English diplomat stationed
in Madrid, he had often looked out through the window at the
French provinces sleeping in the night. "I should have liked to be
the demon Asmodée, you know, the one who raises the roofs of
houses. Nothing in the world has ever appeared to me as mysterious as an old mansion in your country, with its doors and shutters
closed, under the stars. I imagined there unknown dramas, fatal
and hidden passions." There is tragic irony in the laughing re-
joinder of Marcelle that this is a home without a history where
nothing has ever happened or will happen, for at that very moment occurs a *coup de théâtre* which shows how grievously she is
mistaken.

As the play opens we are introduced to this bourgeois dwelling in the pine forest near Bordeaux. Marcelle de Barthas, a widow of thirty-eight, is surrounded by her three children—Emmanuelle just turned seventeen, Anne and Jean, thirteen and twelve respectively—their nurse called simply Mademoiselle, and the enigmatic Blaise Coûture, discharged for incompatibility from the seminary, whose ostensible occupation is that of tutor to the fifteen-year-old son Bertrand. The latter has recently left to spend the summer with an English family whose own son, Harry Fanning, is about to arrive in exchange.

To the surprise of all and the consternation of Blaise, Harry turns out to be not a boy of Bertrand's age but a charming young man of twenty. Insanely jealous of Marcelle's interest in Harry, Blaise prevails upon her to request Harry's return to England. Overhearing a conversation between them in which she expresses her contempt for Blaise and her attraction toward Harry, Blaise Coûture faints behind the door. Wily and with hypocritical humility, he informs Harry next day that it is he, Blaise, who must leave, with the expected result that guileless Harry offers to depart in order to remove the cause of dissension. Under the urging of the children and especially of Marcelle, he changes his mind, however, and to everyone's surprise Blaise actually makes good the threat he had uttered so many times to go away.

Before the final act, which takes place in October as Harry is about to return to England, Marcelle has recalled Blaise and learned from him the brutal truth that it is not herself but her daughter Emmanuelle whom Harry loves. The most poignant scene of the drama shows us her successful struggle to accept this happiness for her daughter rather than push her into the religious vocation to which Emmanuelle had first been attracted. Marcelle is left alone in her solitude, except for the domineering presence of Blaise Coûture, who has reasserted his mastery.

Aside from the poetic setting the greatest claim of *Asmodée* to excellence is its successful portrayal of character with its subtle shading of inner conflict. It is true that Harry Fanning is a highly conventional figure who serves chiefly as a sort of catalyst to arouse the jealousy of Blaise in regard to Marcelle, and that of Marcelle in regard to Emmanuelle. Mademoiselle, likewise, is almost a pathetic caricature in her Griselda-like patience and unquestioning subservience under the harsh cruelty of Blaise. Em-

manuelle, however, one of the most charming of Mauriac's hero-
ines, reveals a delicate analysis of the triumph of love over an
instinctive devotion to Christian mysticism, while Marcelle herself
is a truly Mauriacian study of loneliness and romantic sensibility
in the heart of a middle-aged woman.

Yet thanks to the advice of Bourdet, the essential unity of the
drama is achieved through concentration on the sinister character
of Blaise Coûture. Though he is not a religious hypocrite like Tartuffe, since he was ejected from the seminary for his unconven-
tional beliefs, he bears nonetheless a striking resemblance to Molière's immortal creation, particularly in his efforts to insinuate
himself into the affections of Marcelle by his mingling of divine
and secular love. "I believe . . . it takes two to be able to rise up
to Him, and that we never apprehend Him better than in the
heart of a beloved being who loves you. . . . For many women
the shortest road to perfection is . . . affection." The central motif of Coûture's actions seems to be his almost diabolical need for
dominating those around him. If he shows only boorish rudeness
toward Mademoiselle, it is because she has already yielded herself to him. In his efforts to control and direct the vocation of
Emmanuelle, he is activated less by sensuality than by rivalry
with the *curé* for guiding her future. Unlike Tartuffe, Blaise is
quite frank to admit the infernal power which compels him to
counteract any influence in conflict with his own need for domination. "It is stronger than myself; any influence foreign to mine
in a person dear to me is odious, intolerable. I am seized with a
loathing . . . as if I had discovered finger marks on a white
page." Yet despicable and revolting as Blaise may appear in many
respects, he nevertheless remains a truly human figure in the intensity of suffering which his mad jealously makes him endure.

The success of *Asmodée*, modestly ascribed by Mauriac to
Bourdet and to the stage director Jacques Coupeau, was over-
whelming—a hundred performances that season at the Théâtre
Français, with similar triumphs in Buenos Aires, Rio de Janeiro,
Montevideo, Rome, Milan, Lausanne, and Vienna. A revival in
Paris twenty years later brought the total number of performances
above three hundred. In March, 1938, as I have mentioned, a performance of *Asmodée* in the Bordeaux Opera House by the Comédie Française resulted in delirious enthusiasm and a reconciliation between Mauriac and his native city. As an anonymous critic

remarked, the theatrical season of 1937–38 was for most theater-goers that of *Asmodée.* "Properly speaking there was not a *'querelle'* or battle of Asmodée but rather a prolonged debate, not yet ended. If one did not count himself 'for' or 'against,' still one found around this play that diversity of interpretations, of view-points, of positions, which is the hallmark of living creations." [3]

II Les mal aimés (1945)

Mauriac's second play, *Les mal aimés,* produced at the Théâtre Français during the 1944–45 season, is the author's own favorite, I believe, for he told me he felt he had accomplished here some-thing akin to the work of Chekhov. In the interview in *Conféren-cia* referred to earlier, Mauriac stated that after the success of *Asmodée* he had decided to write a play in which the only atmos-phere would emanate from the characters and their passions, and in which he would conform to the purpose announced by Racine in his preface to *Britannicus,* limiting himself "to an action which, advancing by degrees towards its end, is sustained only by the interests, the feelings and the passions of the personages." When reproached by the critics for his bourgeois *décor,* he claimed that he could easily have transported it to Athens like Cocteau, Girau-doux, and Anouilh had he so wished, but that he wanted to prove to the critics and to himself that his characters existed in them-selves, "that they have enough density to do without everything with which they might be bathed by a novelist and that poetry is, so to speak, only the emanation of the sentiments which possess them." A further ambition of Mauriac in this play was to achieve a style in the theater which would sound direct and natural to the audience and still give the impression of art. It must be admitted that in *Les mal aimés* Mauriac has succeeded admirably in both of these efforts.

The gloomy old mansion in which the scene is laid is occupied by three persons: the sexagenarian father, M. de Virelade, steeping himself in alcohol ever since the desertion of his wife some seventeen years ago; his adored but tyrannized elder daugh-tor Elisabeth, aged twenty-nine; and his younger daughter of sev-enteen, Marianne, whom he detests because of her resemblance to her faithless mother. Elisabeth, whose love for a young medical graduate, Alain, has been thwarted for years by the need to sacri-fice herself to her domineering father, has finally decided to break her bondage and accept Alain's proposal of marriage, unaware that Marianne also is consumed with passion for Alain. When the father discovers that Marianne has been handling the revolver hidden in his desk, he realizes that he now has the means to break up Elisabeth's marriage and keep her chained to him forever. Convincing Elisabeth that her departure with Alain would result in the suicide of her sister, he persuades her to sacrifice herself and force Alain to marry Marianne instead of herself.

In the third and final act which takes place a year later we are not surprised to learn the futility of Elisabeth's abnegation. Marianne, in desperation at her inability to break down the wall of silence which separates her from her husband, comes to implore Elisabeth's aid. While Marianne is in her father's room, Alain arrives. Since Elisabeth has now discovered that her sister had never really contemplated suicide, the two depart in their car to break the bonds which have tied them to Virelade and to Marianne, respectively. Just as Marianne is explaining the catastrophe to her father, Elisabeth returns, unable to persist in her evasion at the cost of so much suffering to others. Life must go on as before, but we feel that these four wretched people are in a treadmill from which there is no escape. Virelade now will never forgive Elisabeth for having thought for a moment of abandoning him. Elisabeth asks with despair how people can ever lay down their burden. "Mine is attached to my shoulders, it is nailed to them securely." Marianne reminds her that she, too, bends under her yoke and that "it is by you that I have been loaded down and crushed." Elisabeth's final words, which end the play, sum up its tragic irony and pathos: "And yet we love one another."

In the view of André Rousseaux, *Les mal aimés*—"this battle of egotists in a cage"—is more noteworthy for the problem it raises than for its characters. In his opinion Mauriac has "never created decisive characters, bearing in themselves a primordial value, but rather agonizing incarnations of a human problem." He feels that the same remark is equally true of Giraudoux, Gide, and Bernanos, with Roger Martin du Gard being the only exception among modern writers. "*Les mal aimés* are a pathetic treatment in depth of Mauriac's great chapter, *Le Désert de l'amour*."[4] It is indeed true that Mauriac has attacked a problem of tragic significance, summed up in Elisabeth's cry of anguish to Alain: "We belong, we are handed over, bound hand and foot, to people who

love us and whom we do not love. Father has taken my life and
Marianne yours. We are their prey until death. One would say
that not being loved creates for them this abominable privilege."
"Yes," Alain replies, "and that those who love each other must be
punished for it."

Yet Rousseaux is wrong, I believe, in his failure to praise the
psychology of Mauriac, for it is the credibility of these lifelike
characters, so human in their frustrations and suffering, which
makes this problem create such tension for the spectator. While
Fowlie has called M. de Virelade only "a slightly transposed figure
of Coûture," [5] he resembles the earlier character, I think, only in
his excessive egotism and tyranny. Less mysterious and diabolical,
he is much more credible in his renunciation of active life because
of despair at his wife's desertion, and in his mixture of selfishness
and adoration toward his elder daughter who, he insists, must be
not only his constant companion but one who is happy in this
servitude. While Alain may appear only a rather helpless pawn in
the struggle between the two sisters, these latter are admirably
differentiated: the younger, Marianne, passionate, avid for happiness, creature of instinct and boundless energy; the elder, Elisabeth, gentle and sacrificial, worn down by long repression in the
service of others until she no longer has the capacity to assert her
right to individual happiness.

Reproached for having presented in *Les mal aimés* "une pièce
noire" in which the prison-like atmosphere is terrifying, Mauriac
replied with a smile, "Isn't life itself terrible?" Yet Pol Gaillard
quotes with approval Mauriac's assertion that only a Christian
could have written this play and adds:

The apologetic value of the plays and novels of M. Mauriac, whose
blackness scandalizes so many devout souls, is in our opinion exactly
the same as that of Pascal's *Thoughts:* to show us man in an odious
light in order to strike down in us the pride of our self-assurance and
prepare our humiliated souls for the coming of Divine Grace, or at
least of the Wager.[6]

In any case it seems likely that *Les mal aimés* will retain its popu-
larity as the play in which Mauriac has approached most closely
the austere sobriety, concentration, and intense emotion of Racine.

III Passage du Malin (*1947*)

For Mauriac's third play, *Passage du Malin,* presented at the Théâtre de la Madeleine in December, 1947, the author states that he has given himself more leeway, less unity of tone, by introducing comic characters—"rather ferociously comic, moreover." He expresses his own fondness for such creatures who would be unbearable if they did not cause us to laugh at them. In Mauriac's view it is easy enough to make people weep, but "comedy is the most difficult thing." The proof of this comment lies perhaps in the failure of this play, by far the weakest in construction and characterization of Mauriac's theater.

There is a certain resemblance in theme between *Les mal aimés* and *Passage du Malin,* for the central protagonist of the latter, Emilie Tavernas, is struggling to free herself from the tyranny of her mother, mother-in-law, unloved husband, and in general from her public image as a coldly efficient director of souls in the Ecole Swetchine which she has founded. As the play opens, we find her trying to protect her former pupil and present colleague Agnès from the approaches of a libertine, Bernard Lecêtre. Her mother-in-law Irma, anxious to bring about a scandal to ruin Emilie's prestige, provides Bernard with a key to Emilie's room, through which he must pass in order to reach his intended victim, Agnès. Finding Emilie even more desirable, however, he seduces her and spends the night in her room before escaping at dawn. Emilie now changes her residence to the school for a week, at the expiration of which she has given a rendezvous to Bernard for her final decision in regard to him. When he appears and learns from her that she feels only shame for her night of love and will elope with him only to avoid the hypocrisy of appearing before her pupils and staff as the virtuous leader and conscience-director, Bernard realizes that he has not succeeded in his effort to win her love. If she should ever shake off her shackles of duty and routine he would come to her at her call, but she replies: "I shall never call you back. One does not leave twice from the prison cell into which I am returning."

The improbability of the plot is evident enough from the résumé just given. The scheme of Irma to cause a scandal for her daughter-in-law, the arrival of Bernard in Emilie's bedroom, the sudden change from Bernard's pursuit of Agnès in the adjoining

room to his seduction of Emilie, the amazing surrender of the latter after a lifetime of respectability—all this makes the play more
akin to a bedroom farce than to serious drama. Not one of the
many characters is really presented in depth, and the two mothers-
in-law who revile each other like fishwives are little more than
grotesque silhouettes. If Mauriac had renounced the theater after
this play it would have been easy to ascribe it to disappointment
over this failure.

IV   Le Feu sur la terre (*1950*)

Yet Mauriac's final play, *Le Feu sur la terre*, has been considered by some critics, among them Claudel and Gabriel Marcel, his
masterpiece, superior to his more successful *Asmodée*. In an article for *La Table Ronde* Mauriac has explained how he came to
choose this title and imagine the theme for this play. He wrote the
drama during the summer of 1949 while watching from his terrace
at Malagar the vast conflagration which enveloped the entire horizon from the Lot and Garonne to the very gates of Bordeaux.
"The fire which was devouring before my eyes the pine trees of
my childhood was transposed into that vast, devouring passion of
Laure, and the characters of my play stood out on the dark red
stage setting of Paul Colin like the calcinated pines on the tawny
sky of my own Guienne." [7]

Deeply impressed by the role in French literature played by
such sisters as Jacqueline Pascal, Lucile de Chateaubriand and
Henriette Renan, Mauriac was inspired in this play by the love of
Maurice de Guérin and his sister Eugénie. To the criticism that
the real Eugénie, so tender, chaste, and self-sacrificing, was far
removed from the devouring passion of Laure for her brother,
Mauriac had answered in advance that he had often wondered:
"If Eugénie had not been that devout girl participating every
morning at the mass and daily nourished by her God, what kind
of woman would she have been? Where would she have found the
strength to consent to Maurice's marriage, in order not to hate her
sister-in-law?"

As the curtain rises old M. de la Sesque, his wife Marguerite,
and their daughters Laure and Lucile are anxiously awaiting the
arrival of their son and brother Maurice, for whom they have
been economizing all these years until the completion of his doctorate in law at Paris. Impoverished by the recent loss of their pine

trees by fire, they hope to arrange the marriage of Maurice with Caroline, daughter of the immensely wealthy Lahures. In Laure's eyes a further reason for this marriage is the apparent docility and insignificance of Caroline, who will represent no obstacle to the renewal of her possessive domination of Maurice which she had exercised all through his childhood.

When Maurice arrives, however, it is to bring the shocking news that he has deceived them all these years and spent their economies on materials for his career as a painter, without ever having crossed the threshold of the university. Still more of a blow to them is their discovery that he has brought with him a wife, Andrée, and their young son, Eric. Even his restitution of the 100,000 francs advanced for his dissertation, plus another modest sum, would have been inadequate to keep the family from turning Maurice and wife and child away from their door, but for the charm of little Eric who reminded them so greatly of the child Raymond they had lost many years before.

The dramatic interest in the following days lies in the frustration of Laure, her desperate attempts to win Maurice away from his wife, encouraged by her discovery that Maurice and Andrée had not gone through a church wedding. In the eyes of the la Sesques, therefore, nothing now interferes with their original project of having Maurice marry Caroline, whose infatuation with Maurice is evident to all. By a surprising tour de force, however, Andrée succeeds in persuading Maurice to undergo a religious wedding, motivated on his part less by vexation against Laure than by resentment at the growing possessiveness of Caroline and her tactless mentions of her rich dowry. Heartbroken on realizing that her hold over Maurice is broken forever, Laure leaves the house in a state of strange exaltation. Fearing that she has committed suicide, everyone sets out to find her, but to the relief of all, Laure finally reappears, resigned with quiet despair to the thought that never more will she have Maurice to herself.

More complicated in plot than *Les mal aimés* because of the greater number of characters and the presence of several subplots, *Le Feu sur la terre* is also less somber. It is true that Mauriac compared the theme to that of *Genitrix* in which we saw a son enveloped by his possessive mother. "Without a husband, without a child, wholly concentrated on her brother, a passionate sister can become in the destiny of this brother nothing but a ferment of destruction." Yet as Claudel pointed out, there is a difference in the jealousy of these two women, for that of Laure is essentially conservative, "expressing the instinct of a group, in the aid of a threatened community."[8] When Jean-Louis Barrault told Mauriac that this play was too discouraging, even more so than the works of Kafka, Mauriac replied that an optimistic ending would have seemed arbitrary and unjustified, and that every time he had tried to give an optimistic denouement to his works the critics had objected and rightly so. "In life I am not at all a man of despair. But it is true that as an author I have little disposition towards hope." Mauriac points out, however, that all his heroes are not so black and that he has "placed in front of Laure a tender and simple young woman, a loving wife in whom many of our women may recognize themselves. I leave to each person the opportunity of adding a fifth act and imagining Laure finally delivered and pacified."

Though the dramatic interest is concentrated throughout on the dark jealousy of Laure, most of the other characters achieve some degree of vividness. This is particularly true of the elderly la Sesque, whose constant preoccupation with money makes him a provincial Harpagon. Claudel, strangely enough, does not find him so odious and ridiculous and considers his indignation over his son's prodigality quite legitimate. Claudel wonders if many of his readers have really understood

the exploit accomplished by Mauriac which places him, in my opinion, in the first rank of our dramatic authors. Anyone can place two actors face to face—it is something quite different to set in motion nine characters, each with his own physiognomy, his own vocation, his own personality . . . so that not one of their concerted movements is without use for the action, for the solution of a truly fundamental problem. . . . It is this tour de force which our friend Mauriac has brilliantly effected and I am happy to shout bravo.[9]

This ardent defense of Mauriac by his friend the great Catholic dramatist Claudel is all the more interesting when we remember his caustic disapproval a few years later of Mauriac's selection for the Nobel Prize.

Not every critic was so enthusiastic. Raymond Cogniat, for instance, found *Le Feu sur la terre* very disappointing, its personages empty of human substance, mere puppets animated not by the torment of their souls but by a mechanical process.[10] More typical, however, of the critics' response was that of Jacques Marchand: "What a rare, beautiful and touching subject Mauriac has brought to the stage." Marchand was clearly impressed by the correspondence between the title and its physical connotation with the psychology of inner conflict.

Le Feu is surely what its author wishes: the minute description of the smothering of a beautiful conflagration; not of its extinction; . . . the description of that moment when the fire plunges underground and pretends to die out, only to surge forth, with treacherous prudence, a little further on.[11]

What, then, is the importance of Mauriac's contribution to the theater, and why did he renounce it, after three successful plays, in favor of a return to the novel? Mauriac himself has never felt that he had brought anything essentially new to the French stage, except perhaps in Les mal aimés, which he likened, as we have seen, to the technique of Chekhov. At the successful revival of Asmodée at the Théâtre Français some twenty years after its first performance it was Gérard Baüer who, in my opinion, summed up most accurately the position which Mauriac holds in the history of French drama. For him, Mauriac was not the herald of a new age but rather the last representative of that bourgeois theater which with Emile Augier and Dumas fils had held the stage for nearly a century and whose knell had been sounded by Giraudoux.

Mauriac is still a writer of bourgeois formation, like Maupassant and Bourget, like Barrès and Loti; and he is perhaps one of the last, just as Thomas Hardy has been in England the last great Victorian novelist. . . . Yes, that sad evening when Mme de Barthas seated herself in resignation before her fireplace marked perhaps a farewell which went beyond her own fate. Mauriac had just brought to the theater, perhaps, in a moving and beautiful work, the model of what it could be no longer. . . . Once or twice more he would be a novelist in the theater; he would not be a new dramatic author.[12]

There is something rather gentle and touching in this valedictory, but valedictory it is, and as such a rather plaintive and poignant occasion. I do not think that Mauriac himself would protest this judgment, for he well knows that his permanent place will be in fiction. In his three successful plays he has been careful to choose his characters from the bourgeois and peasants of the same province he has described so well in his novels and with a minimum of descriptive passages has set before us the strange yet terrifying charm of those isolated dwellings in the fragrant pine forests. If there is anything at all to differentiate his plays from his novels it is their almost complete absence of any religious element, save for brief appearances of a *curé* in *Asmodée* and *Le Feu sur la terre*. In the opinion of Gabriel Marcel it is unlikely that Mauriac abstained consciously from making religion a factor in his plays; "But he may have feared unconsciously to degrade what in his eyes is the highest and most perfect verity by making it a theatrical tool." [13] As Marcel has pointed out, atheism succeeds better on the stage, with the notable exceptions of Bernanos' *Dialogue des Carmélites* and Claudel's *L'Annonce faite à Marie*.

What Mauriac's plays have in common with his novels, besides their characters and setting, is their fundamental pessimism, the hopeless attempts of his protagonists to escape from the prison walls of routine and stark reality which rise up against their dreams, the dreadful loneliness of the individual unable to penetrate and dominate the heart of a loved one. As Mauriac once observed, the title of one of his novels, *Le Désert de l'amour* might well serve for that of his entire work, and this is no less true of his dramatic works than of his fiction.

As early as his third play, Mauriac was beginning to express his nostalgia for the novel, *"mon vrai métier."* He was already hoping to return to his first love, where he could be the sole master of his work, since the play is never entirely what the author has written but depends in such large degree on stage director and actors. What finally induced him to abandon the theater, as he told the present writer, was the death of his beloved friend, M. Bourdet, administrator of the Théâtre Français. "When I lost him, I lost everything," he said. From 1950 on, therefore, we find Mauriac resuming once more, briefly, his function as novelist in spite of dramatic successes which many a writer might well envy.

CHAPTER 8

Literary Influences on Mauriac

I F MAURIAC possesses a uniqueness and originality which make it difficult to compare him to any other writer—even to his great English disciple Graham Greene—few authors, nevertheless, have been so susceptible to so many literary influences. Well versed in the masterworks not only of French literature but also, in translation, of Russian and English literature as well, Mauriac has shared with his readers the impressions these have made on his own concepts of art.

I *Early Influences*

While the "Jammesian strain," the influence of his fellow countryman, the gentle and bucolic Francis Jammes, was clearly evident in Mauriac's first volume of verse, *Les Mains jointes,* more important in his succeeding poetic inspiration was the tortured, mystical spirit of Baudelaire and Rimbaud. Of the latter we have seen perhaps a reflection in the idealist Augustin of his early novel *Préséances,* the young man who exiled himself for a time to Africa. Of the former, Professor Peyre has said, "Mauriac's affinities with Baudelaire can hardly be exaggerated." [1] One of Mauriac's earliest essays had Baudelaire for its subject.[2] In his recent *Mémoires intérieurs* Mauriac has returned to the defense of his beloved Baudelaire, in violent reaction against the spate of Freudian dissections of the poet, of which the latest had been that of Sartre. "Never have I recognized the Baudelaire, the love of my youth, in the sick man analyzed and psychoanalyzed by so many critics and so many famous philosophers." [3] Though Mauriac did not share Baudelaire's antipathy for Musset, it was the former whose influence was paramount in Mauriac's poetry. "The strange thing is that, for my humble part, as long as I wrote verse I have been with all my heart in the direction of Baudelaire . . . that resulted in the poem *Atys* which remains, of all I have written, what disap-

points me the least." [4] For Mauriac *Les Fleurs du mal* possessed a
primordial importance in its influence on all later poets. "From
Rimbaud to Mallarmé and to Valéry French poetry has not devi-
ated from the route opened up by *Les Fleurs du mal*." [5] But more
important for the purpose of this study, not only in his verse but
in his fiction as well in which sin struggles ever with Divine Grace,
Mauriac shows his kinship with Baudelaire's distraught and divided personality. "We know that this sinner belongs to us as the
saints belong to us. The sinner and the saint, as Péguy has written,
form an integral part of the system of Christianity. However
much Baudelaire may deny, his negation always turns into blas-
phemy, that is to say, the act of faith. In truth he never interrupted his prayer. Little does it matter that he did not believe in
the God of philosophers and scholars, or even in that of theologians." [6]

Perhaps the author most dear to Mauriac, from the days of his
earliest immersion in the world of nature in the Landes with their
alternating devotion to Cybele and to Christ, was the tragic young
poet of *Le Centaure,* Maurice de Guérin. "It was he who opened
my eyes to the beauty of the world, but not, as the great Roman-
tics did, to its external beauty; he initiated me into the mute passions of the earth, and gave my hesitant, humble adolescence the
exhilarating certainty that I was the consciousness of inanimate
nature." [7] The brother-sister relationship of Maurice and Eugénie
Guérin fascinated Mauriac (and as we have seen was the inspiration for his last play, *Le Feu sur la terre*) as did the similar bond
of affection between Pascal and his sister Jacqueline.

I have discussed the decisive role which Barrès played in setting
Mauriac firmly on the road to success with his intervention in
favor of Mauriac's first volume of poetry. "After he had collaborated, through his first books, more than any other author in my
formation he intervened so miraculously in my destiny and started
me off." [8] It was Barrès, too, whose influence is most apparent in
Mauriac's youthful novels, particularly *L'Enfant chargé de
chaînes.* At the age of eighteen, when Mauriac had *Sous l'oeil des
barbares* constantly within reach, he felt himself closely akin to
the Barrès of twenty-five years before, even as regards his physical suffering (his chapped hands and feet), the consolation which

Nature brought him, and his contradictory sensation of weakness combined with strength. "The child Barrès, puny and brutalized, decides to become the strongest. What he repeated to himself, wan and clenching his fists, 'They'll see some day,' I used to say to myself." [9] Though this early influence of Barrès' *culte du moi* was to wane in Mauriac's later years when his conservatism gave way to more democratic leanings, he never forgot the debt which his early success owed to the nationalist from Lorraine.

II   *Masters of the Novel*

Balzac was the novelist who delighted Mauriac's youth and was one of those whose pages he opened at random most often in his maturity. "To tell the truth, there is scarcely any other than Proust to give me to the same degree as Balzac that familiarity with an author and the world he created; a work into which one enters and which one leaves without even seeking the beginning of the chapter." [10] Mauriac owed principally to Balzac his decision "to create bonds of relationship between the characters of my first novels," [11] and his ambition to tell the story of an entire family (the reader will recall, for instance, that Fernand and his mother in *Genitrix* had already been introduced in *Le Baiser au lépreux*).

In discussing the advance which the nineteenth century made in the technique of the novel, Mauriac observed that the hero of Balzac is always coherent and unified, that there is not one of his acts "which cannot be explained by his dominating passion, which is not in line with his character." [12] Though Mauriac considers this technique fine and legitimate, he is obviously impressed by the great change which Dostoevski was to introduce into this concept of character depiction, a change to which Mauriac obviously is indebted.

In the midst of the nineteenth century a novelist appeared whose prodigious genius was applied on the contrary not to unravel this skein which is a human creature—who was careful not to introduce a preconceived order or logic into the psychology of his personages, who has created them without expressing in advance any judgment on their intellectual and moral value—and indeed it is difficult if not impossible to judge the characters of Dostoevski, so inexplicably mingled in them are the sublime and the base, the lowest impulses and the highest inspirations. They are not reasonable beings; they are not The Miser, The Ambitious, The Soldier, The Priest, The Usurer; they are creatures of flesh and blood, loaded down with heredities, with stains, subject to maladies, capable of almost anything either of good or evil, and of whom one can expect everything, fear everything, hope for everything.[13]

Mauriac asserts that Dostoevski, the novelist who is the most different from Balzac, "has profoundly marked all of us, or almost all."

Mauriac certainly had his own technique of the novel in mind when he wrote that anyone attentive to the lesson Dostoevski has taught us can no longer limit himself to the formula of the French psychological novel in which the human being is carefully shaped in the rigorous fashion of nature at Versailles. He feels that the problem for the French novelist of today is to deny nothing of the tradition of French fiction and yet to enrich it thanks to the contribution of Anglo-Saxon and Russian writers, in particular of Dostoevski. "It is a question of leaving to our heroes the illogicality, the indetermination, the complexity of living, human beings, and all the same of continuing to construct, to create order according to the genius of our race, of remaining, in short, writers of order and clarity." [14]

Mauriac met Proust only twice before the latter's death. Despite his admiration for this master, Mauriac always felt a lack of moral earnestness and Christian faith in his great work. In his essay *Du côté de chez Proust*, Mauriac expressed this reservation: "God is terribly absent from the work of M. Proust. . . . Merely from a literary point of view, this is the weakness of his work and its limitation." [15] Yet though he feels that he owes nothing to Proust either for his style or for the construction of his novels, he does admit his heavy debt to the author of *Remembrance of Things Past* in other respects.

I had made up my mind not to describe an epoch from the outside. And this is where the influence of Proust has been dominant over me. . . . Proust has fortified and legitimatized this decision, which I should probably have reached even if I had not known *Le Temps retrouvé*, but of which he helped me to become aware; nothing of my epoch would pass through my work without my having found it first inside of me.[16]

Confessing that his own little world of childhood seems very narrow in contrast with the vast world of Proust's genius, yet Mauriac feels himself closely akin to the method Proust used. "I do not observe, I do not describe, I find again; and what I find is the narrow, Jansenist world of my pious childhood, anguished and repressed, and the province which enveloped it." [17] Although Mauriac lived in Paris and knew many kinds of people and milieux, it was as if a door had closed on him at the age of twenty, insofar as the material for his work was concerned. And for these recollections of boyhood, Mauriac did not need to steep in a glass of tea Proust's little madeleine.[18]

In another respect also, in the domain of psychology the influence of Proust on Mauriac was all-important.

Yes, the knowledge of man—in spite of Maritain's warning nothing deters us from going forward, all the more since masters have preceded us in this route and the magic charm which used to forbid the approach of certain subjects has been broken. Proust from this point of view has had a profound influence on all the generation following him. Those mysteries of sensibility from which Maritain bids us avert our gaze, Proust teaches us that it is through them that we shall reach the whole of man . . . it is certain that beyond the social, family life of man there exists a more secret life; and it is often at the bottom of this mud hidden from our eyes that lies the key which delivers him up to us entirely.[19]

The importance of Gide's influence over Mauriac can be felt in the paragraph which begins Chapter XII of his *Mémoires intérieurs:* "There is nothing random in my readings. All my sources touch one another: Pascal, Racine, Gide." [20] Mauriac tells us that in his early days in Paris it was *La Nouvelle Revue Française* which counted most for him; "it was the approbation of Jacques Rivière, Ramon Fernandez, of André Gide especially." [21] From a purely literary point of view, Mauriac considered his work one of the most significant of our time. "For me, *Les Nourritures terrestres, L'Immoraliste, Amyntas* will always remain penetrated with the charm in which the fervor of my twentieth year enveloped them." [22] How warmly Mauriac extols the joy of conversing with Gide, when he had him "under lock and key" at Malagar and during the ten years of the Pontigny meetings.[23]

The most significant event in the relations between Mauriac

and Gide was the latter's famous letter of praise for Mauriac's *Life of Racine*, with its barbed insinuation, as we have seen, that Mauriac was really hypocritical in his attempt to combine Christian piety with an attraction for sinful pleasure. It was this letter which led Mauriac to answer with his self-examination of *Dieu et Mammon*, which even today he considers the most intimate and sincere unfolding of his innermost anxiety and travail. Mauriac feels, however, that if this introspective defense was occasioned directly by Gide's taunt, it was not responsible for the sentiments he expressed, which coincided rather with the religious crisis from which he was then emerging.[24]

There are few writers mentioned by Mauriac more frequently in his essays than André Gide. It would be correct, I think, to call this a love-hate relationship. While Mauriac was susceptible to the attraction of Gide's fascinating personality—"charming, supple, fluid, benign and gracious, prompt to show emotion, capable of effusion, brought by the least trifle to the edge of tears, exquisite in conversation"—most of Mauriac's references to Gide express personal reservations. One of his most frequent complaints—a little surprising in view of Mauriac's confession that he has revealed himself most fully in his novels, and his quotation with obvious approval of Flaubert's remark, "Mme Bovary, c'est moi" —is that "Gide has nothing to disclose to us except André Gide. From the first line of *André Walter* to the last confidence of *Ainsi soit-il* he has explored no other continent than himself." [25] Mauriac believes that *Les Faux Monnayeurs* will only live thanks to the character of Edouard who is Gide himself,[26] and that in general "Gide has brought to perfection the system which consists of drawing glory from everything which defames a life."

For Mauriac, Gide seems to have incarnated a sort of satanic majesty, for no one has wagered his life against Christianity with more coldly rational deliberation. "The extreme importance which Gide has assumed in our personal life comes from this choice, fully conscious of itself, which he made at a moment in his life, a choice as spectacular, if I dare say so, as the wager of Pascal." [27] It was this terrible tranquillity and joy of Gide in reversing the values of good and evil which gave him "the aspect of Lucifer" in the eyes of devout Catholics, intent upon his conversion, among whom was Mauriac (and of course Claudel). Mauriac felt a certain admiration in spite of himself for the dexterity with which

Gide eluded their pursuit as "so lithe in the doublet and under the
cape of Mephistopheles (but was he not rather Faust disguised
with the cast-off frippery of the devil?) he would step over their
bodies and rush off to his pleasures or his readings." [28]

Finally, we should include perhaps in this list of contemporary
literary influences the attack of another "devil's advocate," Jean-
Paul Sartre whose famous arraignment of Mauriac's technique in
La Fin de la nuit is familiar to every student of either author. In
his analysis of that novel Sartre asserted:

> If it is true that a novel is a thing like a picture, like an architectural
> edifice, if it is true that one makes a novel with free consciences and
> with duration, as one paints a picture with colors and oil, *La Fin de
> la nuit* is not a novel—at the very most a sum of signs and intentions.
> M. Mauriac is not a novelist.[29]

Sartre reproached Mauriac primarily for his lack of objectivity, for
predetermining the acts of Thérèse, for his omniscience in de-
scending into her heart to explain her innermost reactions, to
comment upon and judge her conduct. Having in mind no doubt
the sentence with which Mauriac began his treatise *Le Romancier
et ses personnages:* "the novelist is the ape of God," Sartre concluded maliciously: "God is not an artist, nor Mauriac either."
This article of Sartre gave rise to a rather fascinating debate
among literary critics, and Mauriac received warm support from
Nelly Cormeau, P. H. Simon, Majault, and others. Mauriac might
have replied that Sartre's own forte in his *Chemins de la liberté*
was not the creation of living characters, but his answer came
many years later.

> The fact that Mauriac knows what goes on in Thérèse's mind is a
> convention that no novelists escape, even those who think that their
> characters must be known by their words and gestures, without com-
> ment. I have been reproached for judging my heroes and playing God
> with them. Thérèse on the contrary is the being who escapes all judg-
> ment, first of all her own, terribly free at each moment, and watching
> her figure for eternity being outlined at the slightest gesture she may
> risk.[30]

In his last essay on Baudelaire, Mauriac in his turn took issue, as
we have seen, with Sartre's work on Baudelaire, reproaching him

with explaining the poet through physiological means, without awareness of deeper spiritual forces.

Yet Mauriac seems to have borne no malice toward Sartre, and he even admitted later that Sartre's criticism was not without foundation. One wonders whether Mauriac had tongue in cheek when he once wrote that, in composing *La Pharisienne* with Sartre's strictures in mind, he had given greater time and care to this novel than to its predecessors and that, since this novel seemed to have been especially popular in Sweden, it was perhaps to Sartre that he owed his *Prix Nobel*.[31]

III Seventeenth-Century Influences: Racine and Pascal

It will be remembered that of the three "sources" which Mauriac mentioned for his readings, two of them, Racine and Pascal, belong to the seventeenth century to whose spirit Mauriac always felt himself most akin. Once when his friend Bourdet asked him to write a preface for a new production of a play by Corneille, Mauriac refused for the reason that the only writer of the seventeenth century with whom he had no communication was Corneille.

We have seen that Mauriac took part as a child in the production of Racine's *Esther* by the young pupils of Grand Lebrun. "His great figures reigned over me from my childhood; we learned *Esther* by heart in the fifth form, *Athalie* in the fourth, the other great tragedies from the second form on, that is to say at the age of fifteen." [32] For the regret which Mauriac experienced in not having enjoyed under his Marianite teachers the solid literary education of Gide or of the pupils of Alain, he could, however, find consolation in the thought that "the equivalent of what Alain would have taught me to discover among the Greeks, I discovered all by myself in Racine. And what Christian teachers worthy of the name might have taught me, I discovered for myself in Pascal." [33]

The fascination which Racine has always exerted over Mauriac can be deduced from his numerous references to this author in his memoirs, the two essays, and the biography of Racine published in 1928. In his preface to the latter we find the revealing confession: "an author decides to write one biography among a thousand others, only because he feels himself attached to this chosen master; to attempt to approach a man who disappeared centuries

ago, the best route passes through ourselves." [34] This avowal is all
the more poignant when we realize that this biography was written during those years of torment and indecision when Mauriac
was desperately seeking to reconcile his worldly passions and ambition with the austerity of his Catholic faith and Jansenist upbringing. Like the child Mauriac, Racine had been reared in a
somberly pious atmosphere, in which the slightest gestures of
everyday life were governed by this rigorous Christian spirit. "We
know what it is to live, from one's earliest years, in a sort of habit-
ual terror, in the presence of a God whose glance spies even on
our dreams." [35] Seeking to excuse the violence with which Racine
reacted toward his early masters of Port Royal, Mauriac is undoubtedly conscious of his own suffering at the hands of dogmatic
Catholic opponents:

> Today when we do not cease to be a butt for the same attacks which
> exasperated him, we should like to invoke him as a witness; but his
> raillery serves only to confirm . . . that M. Racine had wit, and of
> the most biting kind. Yet this painter of man would have had no
> difficulty in maintaining that it is impossible to make man better
> known without serving the Catholic religion.[36]

Again, do we not see the novelist speaking also for his own creations when he wrote of Racine: "the man who gave such a new
painting of the passions had experienced their fire. For one who
was able to paint love, nothing came from the outside; nothing
new is observed outside ourselves; every discovery is accomplished on our own flesh." [37] And finally, the fact that Mauriac as
early as 1927 was well advanced toward the solution of his own
religious crisis can be seen in his explanation of Racine's reconversion to Jansenism as a result of his despair over the opposition to
his *Phèdre*. "At certain hours of our life, everything in us, and even
the best, leagues itself against God. At other moments, on the contrary, He takes advantage of our misery to attract us to his
paths." [38]

The influence of Racine over Mauriac's literary style can be
seen in the latter's attack on the rhetorical *"ronron"* of Rousseau
and the grandiloquence of Chateaubriand. "Who of us can say
that we are not without this sin, even those (to whom I think I
belong) whom the counter poison of Pascal and Racine had im-

munized from the beginning?" [39] It is not difficult to understand
why so many critics of Mauriac's novels and plays have called
them "Racinian." Like the dramas of Racine, his own fiction and
drama have a burning intensity, a Classical concentration on a
crisis, a pitiless exposure of human frailty and passion, an ambiance of poetry and music. No critic, I think, has ever written a
more perceptive summary of Racine's genius, all the more striking
because it applies with almost equal felicity to Mauriac's own
work.

What belongs to Racine is the rigorous continuity not of a discourse
as in Corneille but of a passion, thought, expressed, clarified, polished,
by a small number of very ordinary words, which compose a music.
Music without dissonance or stressed accordance,—suggestive, to be
sure, but which forbids revery, bound as it is to a reality which is
moreover atrocious. No escape as in Shakespeare, no glance at the
star, never the least respite to turn aside from the present horror and
to meditate calmly on the destiny of other men. We are enclosed in a
cage, between the bars of quite similar verses, facing naked passions
which regard one another and describe one another and which are
told with a lucidity which their fury neither limits nor alters.[40]

And Mauriac concludes that for him Racine is the greatest painter
of human solitude, not that of love but of desire.

Even more far-reaching than the influence of Racine on Mauriac, however, has been that of Pascal, his spiritual mentor from
adolescence to old age. In his *Commencements d'une vie,* it will
be recalled, Mauriac had praised Abbé Péquignot, his professor of
rhetoric, for making it possible for him "to have enjoyed Montaigne, to have glimpsed the contribution of Descartes, and above
all to have cherished Pascal. The Braunschwiecg edition of Pascal,
which never leaves me, is the same I used in rhetoric." [41] In his
essay on Pascal in *Mes Grands Hommes* Mauriac recalls again
lovingly this "book which has accompanied me everywhere since
the year of my second form, torn, yellowed, loaded down with
notes, with fingernail sketches, with photographs, with dates, with
dried flower petals," [42] which he was accustomed to open on certain evenings as an effervescent spring to quench his soul's thirst.
In one of his recent volumes, *Ce que je crois* (What I Believe) in
the final chapter, "My Debt to Pascal," Mauriac avers that Pascal

is the writer to whom he owes the most, who has been his master since his sixteenth year and who remains so today more than sixty years later.

How fortunate for the young lad and his comrades at Grand Lebrun, fledglings just out of the nest on the point of discovering the double universe of knowledge and of passion, was this decisive encounter with Pascal!

This is the instant when Blaise Pascal can save them, especially if they see him as he really was, before his definitive conversion; infinitely different from them in genius and knowledge, but their brother in intellectual pride and in a certain attraction he finds in the passions.[43]

How profound the attraction of Pascal was for Mauriac can be proved by the number of his writings devoted to this beloved master: two volumes, *Blaise Pascal et sa soeur Jacqueline* and *Les Pages immortelles de Pascal;* the first article in his volume *Mes Grands Hommes* (and a second one entitled "Voltaire contre Pascal"); a ten-page article on Pascal's *Les Lettres Provinciales* in his *Memoires intérieurs;* and the final chapter in *Ce que je crois* from which I have just quoted. There are more references to Pascal than to any other author in Mauriac's writings: a glance at the index is enough to reveal thirty-one of these in the two volumes of *Mémoires* and thirty-four in the two of *Bloc-Notes.*

To what extent Mauriac felt himself in accord with Pascal, as well as the few points of view on which he disagreed (or at least thought he disagreed) can be determined from an analysis of these commentaries. First of all, as in the case of Racine, Mauriac in his *Journal* expresses his feeling that a good biographer must experience a certain identity with his subject: "The best biographies are due, almost always, to a certain resemblance between the narrator and the man whose history he writes. . . . We know others only through ourselves and our own secret opens up to us that of the best defended hearts." [44] We recall the severe religious crisis which Mauriac underwent in the late 1920's and his anguished complaint in *Souffrances du chrétien:* "Christianity makes no provision for the flesh, it suppresses it." Then Mauriac discussed the anguish experienced by many excellent priests and others consecrated to God (and undoubtedly by Mauriac himself): "that terror which they surmount but which often oppresses them, of having renounced in vain 'the delightful and criminal accommodation with the world' of which Pascal speaks." [45] Their consolation can be found only in the assertion Pascal attributes to Christ: "Thou wouldst not seek me if thou hadst not already found me." We remember the contrast between the restless anxiety of Mauriac's *Souffrances* and the radiant serenity apparent a few months later in its sequel, *Bonheur du chrétien;* a change visible at the very beginning in Mauriac's quotation of Pascal's comment in a letter to Mlle de Roannes, of Tertullian's remark, "What pleasure is greater than the very disgust for pleasure." Reminding her that the life of Christians need not be a life of sadness, Pascal adds: "One leaves pleasures only for greater ones."

It was at this period that Mauriac, provoked by Gide's letter as we remember, wrote his treatise *Dieu et Mammon* to justify himself not only to Gide but also to his Catholic adversaries. A certain *pensée* of Pascal, to which Mauriac will return many times in his later work, seems to him to clarify the entire debate:

Whatever one may say, one must confess that there is something astonishing about the Christian religion. "It is because you have been born in it" they will say. Far from it; I stiffen myself against it, for this very reason, for fear lest this prejudice beguile me; but although I was born in it, I do not fail to find it so.

Like Pascal, Mauriac was born and brought up in the Catholic religion: "that is my drama." He had tried to criticize it, like Pascal to stiffen himself against it, he envied believers like Psichari and Maritain for whom Catholicism had been a *choice,* but he felt it impossible to escape from it.[46]

In Mauriac's books on Pascal, it is a thoroughly human figure of Pascal that we see emerging. The two aspects of Pascal's nature which appear to have fascinated Mauriac, no doubt because of their peculiar relationship to his own work as a novelist, were his capacity for understanding the innermost nature of man and his firsthand acquaintance with human love, revealed by Pascal's *Discours sur les passions de l'amour.* As a psychologist, Pascal is a true descendant of Montaigne in his delight in the study of man. We may be certain that Mauriac had his own novels in mind when he praises Pascal for having recognized that evil in man demands sometimes "an extraordinary grandeur of soul," a certain

genius usurping the place of God in a man's heart to set in motion
virtues of strength and rashness.[47] It is because of this ability to
understand his fellow man that Mauriac calls Pascal "the only hu-
manist worthy of this beautiful name, the only one who denies
nothing of man . . . the most profound, our brother. . . ."[48]

Whether Pascal himself knew the joys and tortures of love is a
subject which obsessed Mauriac, who returned to it over and over
again. Prefiguring this theme which occurs in all his writings on
Pascal—his certainty that Pascal did not escape the temptations of
human passion—Mauriac wrote: "his excessive distrust, that horror of the slightest caress and the most innocent words, such as
'That woman is pretty,' all that testifies to a life that was long
impure."[49] After reading Pascal's *Discours sur les passions de
l'amour* Mauriac opines that no open-minded critic can fail to find
therein "the involuntary confession, the word which is not invented, the cry of a joy or of a sorrow from which the heart still
bleeds."[50] How well Pascal has portrayed the embarrassment of
a lover, who, after preparing his plan of battle, finds himself
tongue-tied when faced by the presence of his beloved. "When
one is far from one's loved one, one resolves to do and say many
things." Mauriac contends that Pascal has summarized the entire
Proustian concept of love when he wrote that the presence of one
you love is only "a cessation of inquietude."[51]

From this discussion it is but a step to consider whether Pascal
had actually been tempted by vice. How shall we interpret Pascal's statement Christ made to him? "I love thee more ardently
than thou hast loved thy stains." Though Mauriac quotes the assertion of Pascal's sister, Gilberte Périer, that he had always been
free of vice, he obviously gives more credence to Jacqueline's remark that even after receiving Divine Grace Pascal "deserved to
be still importuned by the odor of the morass which you had embraced so zealously."[52] And Mauriac concludes that if purity had
been natural to Pascal he would not have experienced so powerfully a feeling of deliverance.

For completeness it should be pointed out that on two matters,
both related to Jansenism, Mauriac takes issue with his beloved
master. Mauriac is distressed by Pascal's conviction that he belongs to the small number of the elect who have been chosen by
Divine Grace in preference to all others. Such heresy, shared by
Jansenists and Presbyterians, can only be explained by the law

announced by Abbé Bremond: the more terrible the doctrine, the more ingenious is the believer in reassuring himself.[53] Again, Mauriac takes Pascal to task for his dark Jansenist pessimism, which led him to believe that, soiled from birth, we are invincibly drawn into evil for which we are punished by eternal chastisement. Mauriac protests against this doctrine; it is ironic that he himself was accused of the same tendency by Catholic critics: "Here he was entering the open door to heresy; he professed that we are forever reproved for following an invincible penchant, as if, in the material world, it had been a crime for man to be heavy." [54]

These references to Pascal's Jansenism bring us directly to a consideration of Pascal's influence on Mauriac's fiction and theater. When I asked M. Mauriac bluntly whether he considered himself a Jansenist he replied *"Oui et non,"* explaining that he was one with his heart but not with his head. Convinced that a victory for Pascal and Port Royal would have been a disaster for the Church, he reminded me that he had been brought up by a mother who, without ever having read a Jansenist work, was however one at heart; to this day he feels great respect for the Jansenist way of life.[55] In answer to the frequent attacks on Mauriac's novels for their atmosphere of evil passions and moral turpitude, Mauriac has quoted with approval Pascal's affirmation, "a passion cannot be without excess," and he feels that any novelist, obliged to paint the realities of love, ought to place this at the base of his work.

But another statement of Pascal seems to have influenced Mauriac even more deeply. In defining marriage, even Christian marriage, Pascal termed it: "The most perilous and most base of the conditions of Christianity, vile and prejudicial before God." The readers of Mauriac's fiction will recall many examples of this attitude, in such novels as *La Chair et le sang, Le Baiser au lépreux,* and many more. In fact, North can find in all his novels only one example of a truly happy marriage—that of the Puybaraud couple in *La Pharisienne*—a marriage which comes to a speedy conclusion in death. Yet even in this novel North notes this significant passage: "I think that all the misfortune of men comes from not being able to remain chaste, and that a chaste humanity would not know most of the ills with which we are overwhelmed." [56] As a foreword to his novel *Le Fleuve de feu* Mauriac placed, along with similar quotations from St. John and Bossuet, the somber outcry of Pascal: "Woe to the land of malediction which these three rivers of fire embrace rather than water." As a natural corollary to the novelist's dark view of human misery, vice, cruelty, and egotism, we find as solutions in so many novels a sudden intervention of Divine Grace, as in *Le Noeud de vipères, Les Anges noirs*, and others. We are reminded of Mauriac's own reproach to Pascal when we read North's judgment: "Mauriac represents Divine Grace as arbitrary, thus creating the impression that powerless man can be saved only by divine election. This is to misunderstand the doctrine of sufficient Grace and to come close to the Jansenist heresy." [57] Martin Turnell goes even further than North in attributing to Pascal "the poisoned source" in Mauriac's "struggle with the Jansenist virus," the change in the pattern of religion from one "formed by the impersonal, the enduring, the normal" to one "formed by the personal, the fortuitous, the abnormal, until in the end religion itself becomes a single factor in a private world of hatred, lust and guilt." [58] Turnell oversimplifies the case, perhaps, when he finds in Mauriac's Jansenism the explanation for all his shortcomings as a novelist: "It accounts for his poor opinion of human nature, his sense of the nothingness of man, and his lack of charity towards his fellowmen. It also accounts for the unsatisfactoriness of his protagonists and for the unconvincing conversions." [59] Mauriac himself has acknowledged that the criticism in regard to "calumniating and soiling carnal love" is the reproach which "troubles him most."

Whether or not we share the criticism of Mauriac for his excessive pessimism, we may see perhaps in his remarkable gift for rendering his characters vivid and palpable a reflection to some extent of his familiarity with Montaigne, Racine, and Pascal. And in regard to Mauriac's felicity of style and phrasing, there can be no doubt that he looked upon Pascal as his master. For Mauriac, Pascal "appears as the point of perfection attained among us by style and thought. At the same time, the ultimate in depth and in limpidity." [60] In a letter sent out to a subscriber to *La Table Ronde* of which he was then editor, Mauriac emphasized his rule of clarity and simplicity. "Montaigne and Pascal have shown us that one can go very far in the knowledge of man by using the language of simple people." [61] When Mauriac resumed a journalistic career in the 1950's it was to Pascal's *Lettres provinciales* that

he turned to seek the secret "of that verve which, out of an ephemeral debate, has made an eternal debate." [62]

The most succinct and poetic summary of this lifelong association between Mauriac and his master Pascal can be found
in the closing paragraph of his chapter on Pascal in *Ce que je
crois:* "The fire of a single night of Pascal will have been enough
to light one whole life and like the child reassured by the night
light in the room peopled with shadows, because of this fire we
shall not be afraid to go to sleep."

CHAPTER 9

Conclusion

MAURIAC once wrote that the function of a critic is to judge an author on the extent to which he has been true to his own ideals and goals, not to crush him by comparisons with his greater predecessors and contemporaries. Perhaps the analysis of the authors who have most influenced Mauriac has served as an indirect method to which he might not object, for making this comparison and approaching his own ideals and goals. In the rich background of Mauriac's culture we have seen those with whom he has—for a time or always—identified himself. Yet over and above this abundant heritage from which he has drawn there is something unique and special about Mauriac's work which sets him apart from others in the pageantry of French fiction.

Throughout Mauriac's work we have observed three predominant themes, all of them present also in the personality of this most subjective of writers. First, there is the essential element of tension and conflict: sometimes between Cybele and God, passionate and pagan love of nature versus religious faith; sometimes between God and Mammon, worldliness and sensual passion combating the desire for purity and saintliness. Second, we have the desperate loneliness and solitude of the individual, unable to communicate with others, even those most beloved. We recall in this regard Mauriac's own admission that "desert of love" might well serve as title of his entire work. Third, there is the flagellation of bourgeois smugness, social conformity, and lack of true Christian compassion, a theme first appearing in the early *Préséances* but cropping up in most of the later works, particularly in that savage *Noeud de vipères*.

The scathing reproaches of conservative Catholics against Mauriac's works have not been repeated in recent years; as he remarked with a smile, "in comparison with the fiction published since the war, my own novels seem to have been written *à l'eau de rose* [in rose water]." On the other hand, the violent assault launched by Sartre on *La Fin de la nuit* for the novelist's frequent interventions limiting the autonomy of his characters has been followed by a wave of adverse criticism both in France and in England which probably went too far. If some of Mauriac's novels hailed by critics on their appearance now seem flawed and full of weaknesses, the passage of time has allowed a more judicious appraisal and consensus which recognizes at least four masterpieces almost certain to endure—*Genitrix, Le Désert de l'amour, Thérèse Desqueyroux,* and *Le Noeud de vipères*—with two or three others only slightly below them: *Le Baiser au lépreux, La Pharisienne,* and in some respects at least, *La Fin de la nuit.* Similarly, two of his four plays appear to have achieved an honorable place in the repertoire of the theater: *Asmodée* and *Les mal aimés.*

There are of course many valid criticisms to be made against Mauriac as novelist and dramatist; these apply chiefly to his less successful writings but in some cases to his masterworks as well. First of these is his obsession with his own childhood memories. As he himself has said, it was as if a door had closed upon him when he left Bordeaux for Paris at the age of twenty-one—a door which sixty years of life in Paris has scarcely opened. Only one of his twenty novels has its scene located primarily in Paris, *Ce qui était perdu,* perhaps the weakest of his stories. Not only has he returned time after time to the narrow confines of Bordeaux and its environs for his settings—with occasional brief sorties to an unreal and shadowy Paris of dissipation and laxity of moral fiber —but most of his characters have been taken from the hated bourgeoisie and landed gentry of his province. With only a few exceptions such as the lawyer Louis of *Le Noeud,* the world of finance in *Les Chemins de la mer,* Dr. Courrèges in *Le Désert,* does he portray any members of society other than landowners, peasants, or retired capitalists, though a priest recurs frequently among his minor personages.

There is a certain resemblance, too, in these portraits, particularly that of the individual whose consuming passion is dominance over all who surround him or her: Mme Casenave, Brigitte Pian, and in the dramas M. Coûture and M. Virelade. Mauriac himself wonders why this type has been such an obsession for him. In his *Le Roman* Mauriac attempts to justify this reappearance of the same types in various works, stating that it is interesting to see how they would react to dissimilar circumstances. Thus, for instance, he informs us that he took from his father-in-law certain traits both for Fernand Cazenave and for Louis, placing them in entirely different environments. (If he had not mentioned this particular likeness it is doubtful that the reader would have noticed it, and certainly one must admit that the other cases mentioned are far from carbon copies of each other.)

Mauriac composed his novels with almost feverish haste, some of them in only a few weeks. If this is conducive to the dramatic, Racinian intensity of his plots it can result also in rather hurried, unsatisfactory endings, as if the author had tired of his subject and was anxious to wind it up as rapidly as possible; a good example is *Les Chemins de la mer* in which, as in his youthful novels and in *La Fin de la nuit*, the first part is so much better than the conclusion. Another blemish is his occasional descent into melodrama, as in *Les Anges noirs*, a sort of Catholic detective novel, or in the creation of such an operatic and saturnine embodiment of evil as Landin in *Les Chemins*—or even, in the great *Noeud*, the stalking and discovery of the plotters by Louis in Saint Germain-des-Prés.

More important, however, are the reproaches caused by the innate difficulties affecting the Catholic novelist, or as Mauriac would prefer to say, the Catholic who is also a novelist. As we have seen, even such relatively sympathetic critics as North and Turnell have objected to the frequency of miraculous conversions which redeem such diabolic sinners as Gradère in *Les Anges noirs*. To North this seemed like a Jansenist interpretation of Grace, not in keeping with a more orthodox doctrine of "sufficient Grace" or salvation through works. Though this sudden solution does become a little monotonous in Mauriac, I must take issue with the critics who object to the denouement even of *Le Noeud;* it seems to me here that for once Mauriac has carefully prepared the reader for the conversion of Louis, who on so many occasions had perceived a glimmer of spirituality of which his materialistic family remained unaware.

A final criticism, springing also from Mauriac's Jansenist outlook on life, involves the pessimistic and sulphurous atmosphere (the adjective is Mauriac's own) which envelops the world por-

trayed by Mauriac. As he has so lucidly defined himself as a novelist in his Journal II,

I am a metaphysician who works in the concrete. Thanks to a certain
gift of atmosphere, I try to render sensible, tangible, fragrant, the
Catholic universe of evil. That sinner of whom theologians give us an
abstract idea, I incarnate him.

We have seen the result of Mauriac's pietistic upbringing as a
child, his consciousness of his own unattractiveness to teachers
and comrades, his loneliness and solitude. Convinced by Pascal
and Bossuet of the sinfulness of physical love even in Christian
marriage, Mauriac has given us only one example of a happy
wedded life. The impression left by his scathing satire of bourgeois snobbery, conformity, avarice, jealousy, and ambition would
surely convince a Bolshevik reader of the corruption and deca-
dence of Western capitalism. It is this criticism of black pessimism
to which Mauriac has been most sensitive, as we saw in his response to the Nobel Prize in Stockholm in which he attempted to
justify himself by the example of great writers like Balzac and
Dostoevski and by his insistence on the endearing portraits of innocent children in his works. (The only ones that come readily to
mind are little Marie of *Le Noeud* and the noble and pathetic
little Sagouin, though there are indeed a number of appealing
youths such as Jean and Noémi of *Le Baiser,* Luc of *Le Noeud,*
and the luckless lamb of *L'Agneau.*) Mauriac has said that in real
life he is far from being as pessimistic as in his novels and plays,
but that when he tries to create virtuous characters he usually
makes a mess of it. If it is unfair perhaps to criticize Mauriac for
showing us humanity mainly in its baser and more forbidding aspects, it must be admitted, however, that this tendency results in a
certain imbalance and lack of perspective in his works.

The shortcomings mentioned above are serious indeed and
must have been matched by virtues even more impressive to have
assured Mauriac the position in the literary world he occupies today. What specifically are these qualities, in addition to his great
capacity for social satire? We find two of these mentioned in the
reasons which the Swedish jury gave for awarding Mauriac the

Prix Nobel for literature in 1952: "for the *penetrating analysis of the soul* and the *artistic intensity* with which, through the medium of the novel, he has interpreted human life" (italics mine). Perhaps they have omitted the most important factor in Mauriac's greatness—his power of poetic imagination.

There can be no doubt of Mauriac's pre-eminence as an analyst of human motives and emotions and as a creator of characters who stand out in our memory long after we have closed the books in which they appear. From his earliest childhood Mauriac was possessed by curiosity for penetrating into the innermost recesses of those around him—family, comrades, servants, indeed all with whom he came in contact. In twenty novels he was able to return again and again to this rich storehouse of his youth, modified and transfigured by emotions coming from the least noble aspects of the writer's own depths. It is no coincidence that each great novel of Mauriac is called up for the reader by the memory of at least one impelling character who lives on with a life peculiarly his own: Dr. Courrèges of *Le Désert*, the enigmatic Thérèse, the Tartuffe-like Blaise Coûture of *Asmodée*, the possessive Mme Cazenave of *Genitrix*, the unconscious hypocrite Brigitte Pian of *La Pharisienne* and perhaps greatest of all, the sordid miser redeemed in *Le Noeud de vipères*. In them we have a gallery of living portraits of whom any author could be proud.

Artistic intensity—this encomium can be interpreted in several ways. The novels and plays of Mauriac do in fact seize the reader or spectator almost from the opening line and hold him as in a trance. Mauriac's secret here is partly his identification with the struggles of his helpless protagonists, caught in a trap by a fatality closing in upon them, for which the only exit in most cases is death, sometimes ennobled by the sudden illumination of Divine Grace. It is doubtless the anguish endured by the novelist himself, in his own struggle between Cybele and God, between God and Mammon, between his own solitude and his effort to comprehend and find unity in the world about him, which gives an almost feverish intensity to this fictional world. Mauriac's own tendency to intuition and sensation, to composition in the white heat of inspiration, makes him choose a Classic brevity and condensation in the structure of his novels, many of them little longer than a novella or short story in form. It is this starkness of incident and all-consuming flame of passion which make so many critics apply to Mauriac's work the epithet "Racinian."

With the lucidity for which Mauriac is noted, he has himself suggested the quality most likely to make his work endure. He wrote in one of his most recent volumes, *Nouveaux Mémoires intérieurs*:

There was in me, beneath an apparent weakness and perhaps springing from it, a hidden force which will continue to exert itself to my final hour. One word expresses it: I am a poet. Why should I care that others have refused to acknowledge this? For I know that I am a poet and have never been anything else.

Mauriac has repeated this conviction in conversation with interviewers, including the present writer. Obviously he is not referring to his four volumes of poetry, for most of which he now feels little esteem, but rather to his novels and plays. It is this poetic quality which gives such charm to Mauriac's style, full of limpid clarity and musical resonance. It is this gift also which enables him to recapture with such sincerity the atmosphere of his youth, whether it be Bordeaux the city of stone, the moaning pines and burning sand dunes of the Landes, or the verdant arbors and vine-clad hills seen from his Malagar above the Garonne plain. Like Chateaubriand, Mauriac deserves to be called an enchanter. To one familiar with this rather unpicturesque and monotonous region of France, its transfiguration in the mellow memories of Mauriac is almost miraculous. Even his starkest novels, such as *Genitrix*, are embellished by the abundance of metaphors taken from nature, never superimposed as artificial adornment, but always fused in conformity with the actions of his characters. It is Ramon Fernandez perhaps, in his introduction to *Dieu et Mammon*, who has described most acutely this quality of poetic sensation in Mauriac.

Among these sensations it is not the visual ones which dominate. Without doubt he possesses a very precise memory of landscapes, but the predominance of odors, of taste, of tactile sensations experienced or divined is very clear. . . . When one has lived from earliest childhood in this country and among these men, it is by other senses, less material, more subtle, that they are reborn at our call. . . . The cry of a certain bird at a certain hour, the angle of the sun on the pines, the thousand sounds of the Landes, the odor and the contact of beings and dwellings make themselves seen, breathed, heard in a novel of Mauriac. . . .

It is this poetic quality which renders Mauriac's world more tangible and real to the reader than reality itself, which gives Mauriac, I think, his fundamental originality separating him from other contemporary authors, and which accounts in large measure for the spell in which his readers are captured.

Notes and References

(Place of publication is Paris unless otherwise noted.)

Chapter One

1. F. Mauriac, *Memoires intérieurs* (Flammarion, 1959), p. 9. Hereafter referred to as *M.i.*

2. F. Mauriac, "Grève sur le tas" (*Le Figaro Littéraire,* August 10, 1958). Hereafter referred to as *Fig. Litt.*

3. F. Mauriac, *M.i.,* p. 13.

4. F. Mauriac, *Les Maisons fugitives* in vol. *Dieu et Mammon* (Grasset, 1958), p. 261.

5. F. Mauriac, *Commencements d'une vie* (Grasset, 1932), p. 13. Hereafter referred to as *Commencements.*

6. F. Mauriac, *Nouveaux Mémoires intérieurs* (Flammarion, 1965), p. 132. Hereafter referred to as *N.M.i.*

7. *Ibid.,* p. 129.

8. *Ibid.,* p. 130.

9. F. Mauriac, *Commencements,* p. 20.

10. F. Mauriac, *N.M.i.,* p. 130.

11. *Ibid.,* p. 137.

12. *Ibid.,* pp. 140–41.

13. F. Mauriac, *Commencements,* p. 25.

14. *Ibid.,* p. 3.

15. *Ibid.,* p. 5.

16. Raymond Housilane, *La Table Ronde* (January, 1953).

17. F. Mauriac, *N.M.i.,* p. 231.

18. F. Mauriac, *Commencements,* p. 25.

19. F. Mauriac, *N.M.i.,* p. 171.

20. *Ibid.,* p. 172.

21. *Ibid.,* pp. 172–73.

22. F. Mauriac, *Commencements,* p. 29.

23. F. Mauriac, *N.M.i.,* p. 232.

24. F. Mauriac, *Commencements,* p. 29.

25. *Ibid.,* pp. 47–48.

26. *Ibid.,* p. 48.

27. *Ibid.,* p. 53.

28. *Ibid.,* p. 55.

29. *Ibid.*, p. 40.

30. F. Mauriac, *La Table Ronde* (August, 1951).

31. F. Mauriac, *Commencements*, p. 31.

32. F. Mauriac, *N.M.i.*, p. 64.

33. *Ibid.*, p. 234.

34. F. Mauriac, *Commencements*, pp. 67–68.

35. *Ibid.*, p. 81.

36. *Ibid.*, p. 87.

37. *Ibid.*, pp. 110–11.

38. *Ibid.*, p. 117.

39. *Ibid.*, p. 129.

40. F. Mauriac, *Ecrits intimes* (Geneva-Paris, La Palatine, 1953), p. 75.

41. *Ibid.*, p. 78.

42. *Ibid.*, pp. 105–8.

43. *Ibid.*, p. 115.

44. F. Mauriac, *N.M.i.*, p. 236.

45. F. Mauriac, "Cinquante Ans," *Nouvelle Revue Française* (October, 1939), p. 583; also reprinted in *Les Maisons fugitives.*

46. F. Mauriac, *N.M.i.*, p. 237.

47. *Ibid.*, p. 237.

Chapter Two

1. François LeGrix, *Revue Hebdomadaire* (March 11, 1922), pp. 204–14.

2. Amélie Fillon, *François Mauriac* (Malfère, 1936), p. 76.

3. Michael Maloney, *François Mauriac* (Denver, Swallow Press, 1958), p. 176.

4. Edmond Jaloux, *François Mauriac Romancier*, preface to François Mauriac, *Le Romancier et ses personnages* (Editions Buchet/ Castel, 1933), p. 18. Hereafter referred to as *Le Romancier.*

5. Amélie Fillon, *op. cit.*, p. 90.

6. Georges Hourdin, *Mauriac, romancier chrétien* (Editions du Temps Présent, 1945), p. 43.

Chapter Three

1. F. Mauriac, *N.M.i.*, p. 148.

2. Cecil Jenkins, *Mauriac* (Edinburgh and London, Oliver and Boyd, 1965), p. 5.

3. *Ibid.*, p. 79.

4. F. Mauriac, *Souffrances du chrétien* in vol. entitled *Dieu et Mammon* (Editions du Capitole 1928 and Grasset, 1958), p. 97. Hereafter called *Dieu et Mammon.*

5. F. Mauriac, *N.M.i.*, p. 156.

6. Charles Du Bos, *François Mauriac et le problème du romancier catholique* (Editions Buchet/Castel, 1933), p. 67.

7. Fidus, *Revue des Deux Mondes* (June 15, 1933), pp. 787–806.

8. F. Mauriac, *N.M.i.*, p. 161.

9. F. Mauriac, *Dieu et Mammon*, p. 65.

10. P. H. Simon, *Mauriac par lui-même* (Editions du Seuil, 1953), p. 75.

11. F. Mauriac, *N.M.i.*, p. 163.

12. F. Mauriac, *Fig. Litt.* (March 11, 1951).

13. F. Mauriac, *Mémoires politiques* (Grasset, 1967), pp. 14–15.

14. F. Mauriac, *N.M.i.*, p. 241.

15. F. Mauriac, "Le théâtre et l'ideé que je m'en fais," *Annales-Conférencia* (January 15, 1947).

16. Jean Blanzat, *La Table Ronde* (January, 1953), pp. 86–88.

17. Jean Duché. *Fig. Litt.* (November 15, 1952).

18. F. Mauriac, *Le Cahier noir* (Les Presses de Minuit, 1943), p. 31.

19. F. Mauriac, preface to *Sainte Marguerite de Cortone* (Flammarion, 1945).

20. Anonymous, *Je Suis Partout* (March 3, 1944).

21. F. Mauriac, *N.M.i.*, p. 244.

22. *Ibid.*, p. 245.

Chapter Four

1. Quoted by François LeGrix in *Revue Hebdomadaire* (March 17, 1928), pp. 362–69.

2. François LeGrix, *ibid.*

3. Charles DuBos, *op. cit.*, p. 84.

4. Robert North, *Le Catholicisme dans l'oeuvre de François Mauriac* (Editions du Conquistador, 1950), pp. 74–75.

5. Edmond Jaloux, *Le Romancier*, pp. 63–64.

6. F. Mauriac, *Fig. Litt.* (March 11, 1951).

7. *Ibid.*

8. Jarrett-Kerr, *François Mauriac* (Cambridge and New Haven, Yale Press, 1954), p. 58.

9. F. Mauriac, *Le Romancier*, p. 139.

10. Amélie Fillon, *op. cit.*, p. 221.

11. André Billy, *L'Oeuvre* (January 26, 1936).

12. Frédéric Lefèvre, "Une heure avec," *Les Nouvelles Littéraires* (February 15, 1936).

13. Jean Duché, *Fig. Litt.* (July 14, 1951).

14. René Lalou, *Annales-Conférencia* (April 18, 1952).

15. Jean Blanzat, *La Table Ronde* (June, 1952).

16. Interview by Pierre Mazars, *Fig. Litt.* (May 1, 1954).

17. Robert Kanters, *La Table Ronde* (August, 1954), pp. 142–48.

18. Jacques de Ricaumont, *La Parisienne* (May, 1954), pp. 84–88.

19. Maxwell Smith, "My Interview with Mauriac," *Am. Society Legion of Honor* Magazine (Winter number, 1963).

Chapter Five

1. Georges Le Cardonnel, *La Revue Universelle* (March 15, 1922).

2. François LeGrix, *Revue Hebdomadaire* (March 11, 1922), pp. 204–14.

3. Paul Souday, *Le Temps* (March 9, 1922).

4. F. Mauriac, *Le Romancier*, pp. 102–3.

5. Fernand Vandérem, *Revue de France* (January 15, 1924), pp. 389–92.

6. Edmond Jaloux, *Le Romancier*, p. 32.

7. *Ibid.*, p. 40.

8. F. Mauriac, *Le Romancier*, pp. 127–28.

9. Cecil Jenkins, Introduction to ed. of *Thérèse Desqueyroux* (Univ. of London Press, London, 1964), pp. 22–26.

10. F. Mauriac, *Le Romancier*, p. 110.

11. Edmond Jaloux, *ibid.*, pp. 42–50.

12. John Charpentier, *Mercure de France* (April 15, 1922), pp. 416–28.

13. F. Mauriac, "Vue sur mes romans," *Fig. Litt.* (November 5, 1952).

14. Cecil Jenkins, Introduction to *Thérèse Desqueyroux*, pp. 26–28.

15. Henri Peyre, *French Novelists of Today* (Oxford Univ. Press, New York, 1967), pp. 112–13.

16. F. Mauriac, *Le Romancier*, p. 124.

17. F. Mauriac, *Fig. Litt.* (November 5, 1952).

18. Albert Cahuet, *L'Illustration* (February 2, 1935), p. 149.

19. Edmond Jaloux, *Les Nouvelles Littéraires* (February 2, 1935).

20. Henri Peyre, *op. cit.*, p. 113.

21. F. Mauriac, *Le Romancier*, pp. 111, 112.

22. F. Mauriac, "Vue sur mes romans," *Fig. Litt.* (November 15, 1952).

23. F. Mauriac, *Le Romancier*, p. 132.

24. Martin Turnell, *The Art of French Fiction* (New Directions, Norfolk, Conn., 1959), p. 345.

25. Nelly Cormeau, *L'Art de François Mauriac* (Grasset, 1951), p. 164.

26. Jacques Robichon, *François Mauriac* (Etudes Universitaires, Paris and Brussels, 1953), p. 109.

Chapter Six

1. Marius Richard, *Revue de France* (May 1, 1938).
2. André Thérive, *Temps Présent* (March 11, 1938).

Chapter Seven

1. B. Dorival, *La Vie Intellectuelle* (January 25, 1938), pp. 294–309.
2. F. Mauriac, "Le Théâtre," *Annales-Conférencia* (January 15, 1947).
3. *Revue Hebdomadaire* (July 9, 1938), pp. 234–35.
4. André Rousseaux, *Fontaine* (April, 1945), p. 248.
5. Wallace Fowlie, *Dionysus in Paris* (Meridian Books, New York, 1961), p. 153.
6. Pol Gaillard, *La Pensée,* nouvelle série (January–March, 1945), pp. 110–14.
7. F. Mauriac, *La Table Ronde* (November, 1950).
8. Paul Claudel, *Fig. Litt.* (November 25, 1950).
9. *Ibid.*
10. Raymond Cogniat, *Arts* (November 17, 1950).
11. Jacques Marchand, *Fig. Litt.* (November 11, 1950).
12. Gérard Baüer, *La Vie Parisienne* (May, 1956), pp. 13–15.
13. Gabriel Marcel, *La Table Ronde* (January, 1953), pp. 125–30.

Chapter Eight

1. Henri Peyre, *op. cit.*, p. 160, note 6.
2. Available in English translation in *Twentieth Century Views* (Prentice Hall, New York, 1962).
3. F. Mauriac, *M.i.*, p. 48.
4. *Ibid.*, p. 56.
5. *Ibid.*, p. 55.
6. *Ibid.*, p. 51.
7. F. Mauriac, *Second Thoughts* (The World Publishing Co., Cleveland, Ohio, 1961), p. 76.
8. F. Mauriac, *M.i.*, p. 124.
9. *Ibid.*, p. 125.
10. *Ibid.*, p. 61.
11. F. Mauriac, "Vue sur mes romans," *Fig. Litt.* (November 15, 1952).
12. F. Mauriac, *Le Roman* (Artisan du Livre, 1928), pp. 47–48.
13. *Ibid.*, pp. 49–50.
14. *Ibid.*, pp. 54–55.
15. *Ibid.*, p. 70. Also in F. Mauriac, *Proust's Way* (Philosophical Library, New York, 1950), p. 46.

16. F. Mauriac, "Vue sur mes romans," *Fig. Litt.* (November 15, 1952).

17. *Ibid.*

18. F. Mauriac, *M.i.*, p. 14.

19. F. Mauriac, *Le Roman*, pp. 42–44.

20. F. Mauriac, *M.i.*, p. 173.

21. F. Mauriac, *N.M.i.*, p. 239.

22. F. Mauriac, *M.i.*, p. 182.

23. *Ibid.*, p. 186.

24. *Ibid.*, p. 247.

25. *Ibid.*, p. 107.

26. *Ibid.*, p. 108.

27. *Ibid.*, p. 180.

28. *Ibid.*, p. 185.

29. Jean-Paul Sartre, "F. Mauriac et la liberté," reprinted in *Situations I* (Gallimard, 1947), pp. 56–57.

30. F. Mauriac, "Vue sur mes romans," *Fig. Litt.* (November 15, 1952).

31. F. Mauriac, *M.i.*, p. 208.

32. *Ibid.*, p. 166.

33. F. Mauriac, *N.M.i.*, p. 207.

34. F. Mauriac, *Vie de Jean Racine* (Plon, 1928), p. 8.

35. *Ibid.*, p. 11.

36. *Ibid.*, p. 46.

37. *Ibid.*, p. 50.

38. *Ibid.*, p. 90.

39. F. Mauriac, *N.M.i.*, p. 218.

40. F. Mauriac, *M.i.*, pp. 162–63.

41. F. Mauriac, *Commencements*, pp. 55–56.

42. F. Mauriac, *Mes Grands Hommes* (Editions du Rocher, Monaco, 1944), pp. 1–3.

43. *Ibid.*, pp. 4–5.

44. F. Mauriac, *Journal I* (Grasset, 1942), p. 211.

45. F. Mauriac, *Souffrances du chrétien* in *Dieu et Mammon*, p. 107.

46. *Ibid.*, pp. 19–20.

47. F. Mauriac, *Blaise Pascal et sa soeur Jacqueline* in *Oeuvres Complètes*, Vol. VIII (Grasset, chez Fayard, 1950), p. 258.

48. *Ibid.*, pp. 298–99.

49. F. Mauriac, *Dieu et Mammon*, pp. 157–58.

50. F. Mauriac, *Les Pages immortelles de Pascal* (Editions Buchet/Castel, 1947), p. 15.

51. F. Mauriac, *Blaise Pascal et sa soeur Jacqueline* in *Oeuvres Complètes*, Vol. VIII (Grasset, chez Fayard, 1950), p. 204.

52. F. Mauriac, *Les Pages immortelles de Pascal*, p. 20.

53. F. Mauriac, *Blaise Pascal et sa soeur Jacqueline* in *Oeuvres Complètes*, Vol. VIII (Grasset, chez Fayard, 1950), p. 175.

54. F. Mauriac, *Les Pages immortelles de Pascal,* p. 10.

55. Maxwell Smith, "My Interview with Mauriac," *Am. Soc. Legion of Honor Magazine* (Winter number 2, 1963).

56. Robert North, *op. cit.,* pp. 102–22.

57. *Ibid.*

58. Martin Turnell, *op. cit.,* p. 360.

59. *Ibid.,* p. 346.

60. F. Mauriac, *Ce que je crois* (Grasset, 1962), p. 38.

61. F. Mauriac, *Lettres ouvertes* (Editions du Rocher, Monaco, 1952), p. 70.

62. F. Mauriac, *Ce que je crois,* p. 144.

Selected Bibliography

PRIMARY SOURCES

Collected Works: The place of publication
is Paris unless otherwise noted.

Oeuvres complètes de François Mauriac (Grasset: chez Fayard).
The Collected Edition of the Novels of François Mauriac, tr. Gerard
Hopkins, 17 vols. (London: Eyre and Spottiswoode, 1946–61).

Fiction

L'Enfant chargé de chaînes (Grasset, 1913). Eng. tr. *Young Man in
Chains,* tr. Gerard Hopkins (London: Eyre and Spottiswoode,
1961; and New York: Farrar, Straus, 1963).

La Robe prétexte (Grasset, 1914). Eng. tr. *The Stuff of Youth,* tr.
Gerard Hopkins (London: Eyre and Spottiswoode, 1960).

La Chair et le sang (Emile-Paul, 1920). Eng. tr. *Flesh and Blood,*
tr. Gerard Hopkins (London: Eyre and Spottiswoode, 1954; and
New York: Farrar, Straus, 1955; also, Dell paperback edition).

Préséances (Emile-Paul, 1921). Eng. tr. *Questions of Precedence,* tr.
Gerard Hopkins (London: Eyre and Spottiswoode, 1958; and
New York: Farrar, Straus, 1959).

Le Baiser au lépreux (Grasset, 1922; also Collection Pourpre and
Livre de Poche). Eng. tr. *A Kiss for the Leper,* with *Genitrix,*
tr. Gerard Hopkins (London: Eyre and Spottiswoode, 1950).

Le Fleuve de feu (Grasset, 1923, and Collection Pourpre). Eng. tr.
The River of Fire, tr. Gerard Hopkins (London: Eyre and
Spottiswoode, 1954).

Genitrix (Grasset, 1923, and Club Pourpre—Fayard—1952). Eng.
tr. *Genitrix,* tr. Gerard Hopkins (London: Eyre and Spottiswoode, 1950).

Le Désert de l'amour (Grasset, 1925; also Collection Pourpre and
Livre de Poche). Eng. tr. *The Desert of Love,* with *The Enemy,*
tr. Gerard Hopkins (London: Eyre and Spottiswoode, 1949; and
New York: Pellegrini and Cudahy, 1951).

Thérèse Desqueyroux (Grasset, 1927; also Collection Pourpre and
Livre de Poche). Eng. tr. *Thérèse,* tr. Gerard Hopkins (London:

Eyre and Spottiswoode, 1947; New York: Holt, 1947; and Farrar, Straus, 1951. Also Doubleday, Anchor; and Penguin editions).

Destins (Grasset, 1928). Eng. tr. *Lines of Life,* tr. Gerard Hopkins (London: Eyre and Spottiswoode, 1957; and New York: Farrar, Straus, 1957).

Trois Récits (Grasset, 1929).

Ce qui était perdu (Grasset, 1930). Eng. tr. *That Which Was Lost,* with *The Dark Angels,* tr. J. H. F. McEwen (London: Eyre and Spottiswoode, 1950).

Le Noeud de vipères (Grasset, 1932; also Collection Pourpre and Livre de Poche). Eng. tr. *The Knot of Vipers,* tr. Gerard Hopkins (London: Eyre and Spottiswoode, 1951); also as *Vipers Tangle,* tr. W. B. Welles (London: Gollancz, 1933; New York: Sheed and Ward, 1933 and 1937, and Doubleday Image edition).

Le Mystère Frontenac (Grasset, 1933; also Collection Pourpre and Livre de Poche). Eng. tr. *The Frontenac Mystery,* tr. Gerard Hopkins (London: Eyre and Spottiswoode, 1952); and *The Frontenacs* (New York: Farrar, Straus, 1961).

La Fin de la nuit (Grasset, 1936; also Collection Pourpre and Livre de Poche). Eng. tr. *The End of the Night* in *Thérèse,* tr. Gerard Hopkins (London: Eyre and Spottiswoode, 1947).

Les Anges noirs (Grasset, 1936; also Collection Pourpre and Livre de Poche). Eng. tr. *The Dark Angels,* with *That Which Was Lost,* tr. Gerard Hopkins (London: Eyre and Spottiswoode, 1950).

Plongées (Grasset, 1938).

Les Chemins de la mer (Grasset, 1939). Eng. tr. *The Unknown Sea,* tr. Gerard Hopkins (London: Eyre and Spottiswoode, 1948; and New York: Farrar, Straus, 1948; also in Penguin edition).

La Pharisienne (Grasset, 1941). Eng. tr. *A Woman of the Pharisees,* tr. Gerard Hopkins (London: Eyre and Spottiswoode, 1946; and New York: Farrar, Straus, 1946; also Doubleday Image edition).

Le Sagouin (Paris-Geneva: La Palatine-Plon, 1951, and Livre de Poche). Eng. tr. *The Little Misery,* tr. Gerard Hopkins (London: Eyre and Spottiswoode, 1952).

Galigaï (Flammarion, 1952). Eng. tr. *The Loved and the Unloved,* tr. Gerard Hopkins (London: Eyre and Spottiswoode, 1953; and New York: Pellegrini and Cudahy, 1952).

L'Agneau (Flammarion, 1954). Eng. tr. *The Lamb,* tr. Gerard Hopkins (London: Eyre and Spottiswoode, 1955; and New York: Farrar, Straus, 1956; also Noonday edition).

Un adolescent d'autrefois (Flammarion, 1969).

Plays

Asmodée (Grasset, 1938). Eng. tr. *Asmodée, or The Intruder*, tr. Basil Bartlett (London: Secker and Warburg, 1939; and Toronto: Saunders, 1939).
Les mal aimés (Grasset, 1945).
Passage du Malin (La Table Ronde, 1945).
Le Feu sur la terre (Grasset, 1951).

Poetry

Les Mains jointes (Falque, 1909).
L'Adieu a l'adolescence (Stock, 1911).
Orages (Champion, 1925).
Le Sang d'Atys (Grasset, 1940).

Biographies

La Vie de Jean Racine (Plon, 1928).
Blaise Pascal et sa soeur Jacqueline (Hachette, 1931; also in Vol. VIII of *Oeuvres complètes*, Grasset).
La Vie de Jésus (Flammarion, 1936).
Sainte Marguerite de Cortone (Flammarion, 1945). Eng. tr. *Margaret of Cortona*, tr. Barbara Wall (London: Burns Oates and Washbourne, 1948) and *Saint Margaret of Cortona*, tr. Bernard Frechtman (New York: Philosophical Library, 1948).
Les Pages immortelles de Pascal (Corrêa, 1947).
De Gaulle (Grasset, 1964).

Autobiographical or Literary Criticism

Bordeaux (Emile-Paul, 1926).
Le Roman (Artisan du Livre, 1928).
Dieu et Mammon (Editions du Capitole, 1929; and Grasset, 1958); contains also *Souffrances et bonheur du chrétien*, 1931. Eng. tr. *God and Mammon*, tr. Bernard and Barbara Wall (London and New York: Sheed and Ward, 1936).
Trois grands hommes devant Dieu (Editions du Capitole, 1930). On Molière, Rousseau, and Flaubert.
Le Romancier et ses personnages (Editions Buchet/Castel, 1933).
Journal, Vols. 1–4 (Grasset, 1934–53).
Le Cahier noir (Editions de Minuit, 1943); also published in English and French as *The Black Note Book* (London: Burrop, Matthieson, 1944).
Les Pages immortelles de Pascal (Editions Buchet/Castel, 1947).
Mes grands hommes (Monaco: Editions du Rocher, 1949). Eng. tr.

Men I Hold Great, tr. Elsie Pell (London: Rockliff, 1952), and
as *Men I hold Great* (New York: Philosophical Library, 1951).
On Pascal, Molière, Chateaubriand, Balzac, Flaubert, and others.

Ecrits intimes (Geneva-Paris: La Palatine, 1953). Includes *Commencements d'une vie, Bordeaux, Ma rencontre avec Barrès* and
Journal d'un homme de 30 ans.

Bloc-Notes, 1952–57 (Flammarion, 1958).

Mémoires intérieurs (Flammarion, 1959). Eng. tr. by Gerard Hopkins
(London: Eyre and Spottiswoode, 1960; and New York: Farrar,
Straus, 1961).

Le Nouveau Bloc-Notes, 1958–60 (Flammarion, 1961).

Ce que je crois (Grasset, 1962). Eng. tr. *What I Believe,* tr. Wallace
Fowlie (New York: Farrar, Straus, 1963).

Nouveaux Mémoires intérieurs (Flammarion, 1965). Eng. tr. *The
Inner Presence,* tr. by Herma Briffault (Indianapolis, Kansas
City, and New York: The Bobbs Merrill Co., 1968).

Mémoires politiques (Grasset, 1967).

SECONDARY SOURCES

Books

CORMEAU, NELLY. *L'Art de François Mauriac* (Grasset, 1951). The
book which Mauriac himself considered the most perceptive and
comprehensive; scholarly but extremely eulogistic.

DuBos, CHARLES. *François Mauriac et le problèm du romancier catholique* (Editions Buchet/Castel, 1933). The eulogy of a close friend
who felt that Mauriac had finally attained, as a result of his
religious crisis and reconversion, perfection as a Catholic novelist.

FILLON, AMÉLIE. *François Mauriac* (Malfère, 1936). Stimulating and
original, one of the best of early appreciations of his novels.

FLOWERS, J. E. *Intention and Achievement: A Study of the Novels
of François Mauriac* to be published by the Clarendon Press
(England), Nov., 1969.

GRALL, XAVIER. *François Mauriac, journaliste* (Editions du Cerf,
1960). As the title indicates, concerned only with Mauriac's
career as journalist, well presented here.

HOURDIN, GEORGES. *Mauriac, romancier chrétien* (Editions du Temps
Présent, 1945). A not overly favorable appreciation of Mauriac
from a Catholic viewpoint.

JARRETT-KERR, MARTIN. *François Mauriac* (Cambridge, also Yale
Univ. Press, 1954). Mauriac viewed in this brief book rather
harshly, from a purely Anglican standpoint.

JENKINS, CECIL. *Mauriac* (Oliver and Boyd, London and Edinburgh,
1965). Highly recommended for students, perhaps the best brief

treatment yet to appear; succinct, clear, fair, and well-balanced, though I think overcritical of his dramas.

MAJAULT, JOSEPH. *Mauriac et l'art du roman* (Robert Laffont, 1946). Sympathetic but on the whole a fair and well-documented presentation.

MALONEY, MICHAEL F. *François Mauriac* (Swallow Press, Denver, 1958). Brief but excellent treatment, particularly of Mauriac's fusion of poetic imagery with action.

NORTH, ROBERT J. *Le Catholicisme dans l'oeuvre de François Mauriac* (Editions du Conquistador, 1950). Penetrating study by a Catholic critic, particularly of Mauriac's Jansenist tendencies.

PALANTE, ALAIN. *Mauriac, le roman et la vie* (Editions Le Portulan, 1946). The author's thesis is that all Mauriac's work, like that of Proust, rests on poetic introspection. He insists, however, on the limitations of Mauriac's art as novelist.

RADEAU, EMILE. *Comment lire François Mauriac* (Editions Aux Etudiants de France, 1945). A carefully balanced summary of Mauriac's virtues and shortcomings as a novelist.

ROBICHON, J. *François Mauriac* (Editions Universitaires, 1958). Excellent concentrated analysis of the novelist.

SIMON, PIERRE-HENRI. *Mauriac par lui-même* (Editions du Seuil, 1953). Like other volumes in its series, valuable for its documentation, its many photographs, typical quotations from Mauriac, and brief excerpts from his works.

General Articles in Books and Magazines

ALBÉRÈS, R. M. "Mauriac et le romantisme chrétien" (*La Parisienne*, May, 1956), pp. 6–11. The critic sees in Mauriac's work primarily an expression of Christian Romanticism which the Romantic period had lacked. This issue contains many valuable articles on Mauriac, including one by Gérard Baüer.

BRÉE, GERMAINE and GUITON, MARGARET. *The French Novel from Gide to Camus* (Harcourt, Brace and World, N. Y. and Burlingame, 1962); originally published under the title *An Age of Fiction* by Rutgers Univ. Press, 1957, pp. 113–22. Excellent introduction for the student.

FERNANDEZ, RAMON. Preface to second edition of *Dieu et Mammon* (Catalogne, 1935). Enthusiastic and perceptive discussion of Mauriac's art as a novelist.

FIDUS (*Revue des Deux Mondes*, June 15, 1933), pp. 787–806. Fascinating evocation of Mauriac's personality against the background of his native Bordeaux and country estate.

FOWLIE, WALLACE. *Dionysus in Paris* (Meridian Books, New York, 1961), pp. 147–57. A discussion of Mauriac's dramatic works.

JALOUX, EDMOND. Preface to *Le Romancier et ses personnages* (Corrêa, 1933). Contains all the reviews of Mauriac's novels by this perceptive critic up to this date. Extremely useful for the study of Mauriac.

MARCEL, GABRIEL. "Notes sur le théâtre de François Mauriac" (*La Table Ronde*, No. 61, Jan., 1953). Excellent appraisal of Mauriac's contribution to the theater. This special number includes articles also by Nelly Cormeau on Mauriac's poetry, by P. A. Lesort on his novels, and others.

PEYRE, HENRI. *French Novelists of Today* (Oxford Univ. Press, New York, 1967), pp. 101–21; also published earlier in his *The Contemporary French Novel* (Oxford Univ. Press, New York, 1955), pp. 101–21. As is the case with other chapters in this work, an extremely comprehensive, perceptive, and well-balanced appreciation, of great value for the student of Mauriac.

SARTRE, JEAN PAUL. "Mauriac et la liberté" (*Nouvelle Revue Française I*, 1939), pp. 212–32, reprinted in *Situations I* (Gallimard, 1947), pp. 36–57. Sartre's famous and controversial attack on Mauriac's lack of freedom for his characters.

SMITH, MAXWELL A. "My Interview with Mauriac" (*American Society Legion of Honor Magazine*, No. 2, Winter, 1963). Contains many frank comments by Mauriac concerning his novels and plays.

SMITH, MAXWELL A. "The Theater of François Mauriac" (*American Society Legion of Honor Magazine*, Spring, 1966). A discussion of Mauriac's contribution to modern French drama and his reasons for reverting to fiction.

TURNELL, MARTIN. *The Art of French Fiction* (New Directions, Norfolk, Conn., 1959), pp. 287–360. A stimulating but provocative and tendentious essay, blaming Mauriac's pessimism on the "poison" of Jansenism and his inheritance from Pascal.

Index